D0501685

Shakespeare—
Who Was He?

SHAKESPEARE—
Who Was He?

The Oxford Challenge to the Bard of Avon

RICHARD F. WHALEN

Foreword by Paul H. Nitze

Westport, Connecticut
London

Library of Congress Cataloging-in-Publication Data

Whalen, Richard F.
    Shakespeare—who was he? : the Oxford challenge to the Bard of
Avon / Richard F. Whalen ; foreword by Paul H. Nitze.
        p.   cm.
    Includes bibliographical references (p.   ) and index.
    ISBN 0–275–94850–1
        1. Shakespeare, William, 1564–1616—Authorship—Oxford theory.
    2. Oxford, Edward de Vere, Earl of, 1550–1604—Authorship.
    3. Dramatists, English—Early modern, 1500–1700—Biography.
    4. Nobility—Great Britain—Biography.   5. Drama—Authorship.
    I. Title.
    PR2947.09W43   1994
    822.3'3—dc20   94–11303

British Library Cataloguing in Publication Data is available.

Copyright © 1994 by Richard F. Whalen

All rights reserved. No portion of this book may be
reproduced, by any process or technique, without the
express written consent of the publisher.

Library of Congress Catalog Card Number: 94–11303
ISBN: 0–275–94850–1

First published in 1994

Praeger Publishers, 88 Post Road West, Westport, CT 06881
An imprint of Greenwood Publishing Group, Inc.

Printed in the United States of America

The paper used in this book complies with the
Permanent Paper Standard issued by the National
Information Standards Organization (Z39.48–1984).

10 9 8 7 6

Copyright Acknowledgments

The author and publisher gratefully acknowledge permission to reprint previously copyrighted material:

The six signatures attributed to Shakespeare, by permission of the Shakespeare Oxford Society.

Illustrations 2, 3 and 4, by permission of the Folger Shakespeare Library.

Every reasonable effort has been made to trace the owners of copyright materials in this book, but in some instances this has proven impossible. The author and publisher will be glad to receive information leading to more complete acknowledgments in subsequent printings of the book and in the meantime extend their apologies for any omissions.

Contents

Foreword

Some forty-five years ago I served in the U.S. State Department with Charlton Ogburn. At that time, he was stationed in Jakarta, Indonesia, and had strong views about the future of the French and Dutch colonial regimes in Southeast Asia.

He also had strong views about the Shakespeare authorship question. He persuaded me that it was improbable that the man from Stratford-on-Avon could have written Shakespeare's works and much more probable that they had sprung from the pen of Edward de Vere, earl of Oxford. During the intervening years much new information has come to light, the Oxfordian hypothesis has been strengthened, and Charlton Ogburn published his landmark book. I believe the considerations favoring the Oxfordian hypothesis, as presented by him and by Richard Whalen, president of the Shakespeare Oxford Society, are overwhelming.

I have devoted most of my life to the practice and theory of politics. For me, Shakespeare is the supreme commentator on the human condition and the realities of the political society in which men and women must live. In dramatic poetry of unsurpassed force and beauty he shows us the tension between the aspirations of the individual and the constraints of society. Human passions that ignore these constraints have fatal results.

Overweening ambition contains the seeds of its own destruction. A rigid sense of justice untempered by mercy fails to achieve its goal. Folly in high places must be exposed and cleansed for the good of society. Political power must be used judiciously or it leads to defeat.

No other writer, no political philosopher has surpassed Shakespeare's extraordinary insight into the moral and political problems that beset individuals in a society of laws, customs, and conflicting needs and ambitions. As settings for his human dramas he almost always picks the highest levels of political power. There he applies his profound poetic genius to explore the passions of kings, queens, emperors, princes, dukes, and counts, the power they exercise, the policies they enforce, and the moral dilemmas they face. Rulers are his greatest heroes.

Shakespeare knows what it is like at the center of power. He has the insider's knowledge of the way power can be used for good or for evil and the consequences that ensue. He understands the struggles that result from the tension between ideals of morality and the needs of statecraft. Even Walt Whitman, no member of the power elite but an acute student of the human condition and "poet of the common man," observed in a flash of insight more than a century ago that only one of the "wolfish earls," an aristocrat of the ruling class, could have written the history plays. Political leaders as diverse as Abraham Lincoln and Otto von Bismarck have turned to Shakespeare for instruction, and probably consolation.

It's fashionable today to declare "the death of the author"; the author's life and experience count for nought. Any consideration of the author's intention or meaning is rejected. Rejected, too, is any thought that the author was communicating something important to the spectator or the reader. For those afflicted by this fashionable myopia, who Shakespeare was, how he lived, and what he was trying to tell us are irrelevant. But fashions come and go, and I am told there are signs that the negation of authorial intention in academic literary criticism has peaked.

For Richard Whalen, Shakespeare lives. And he lives in the person of Edward de Vere, seventeenth earl of Oxford, an Elizabethan poet, playwright, and patron of acting companies who seems eminently qualified to have written the works of Shakespeare. Oxford was one of Whitman's "wolfish earls." He was a member of Queen Elizabeth's court and son-in-law of her principal adviser. References to his life are found throughout the works of Shakespeare.

In the long-running controversy over Shakespeare's identity, Oxford has been gaining ground. Magazine articles and TV programs have examined the evidence. Even the Folger Shakespeare Library has seen fit to recognize the claims for Oxford in one of its exhibitions, although it is not yet ready to accept the possibility of his authorship.

In his analysis of the controversy, Whalen has tried to be as objective as possible, total objectivity being impossible. He has distilled the essence of the arguments for both the earl of Oxford and the man from Stratford. His presentation of the case for the Stratford man may be the most complete that is available. His careful analysis of the arguments, however, demonstrates that the case for Oxford is most persuasive.

It's a fascinating controversy. Some call it the greatest of all literary problems. In a clear, concise, eminently readable style, Whalen takes the reader on a most entertaining and instructive tour of the great debate. Much has been written on the Shakespeare authorship question, but Whalen's brisk summary of it should lead to a much wider understanding of the surprisingly strong case for Oxford and the shaky foundation under the pedestal of the Bard of Avon.

The question of the true identity of Shakespeare the man, the poet, the playwright, the supreme commentator on society and the human condition should not be confined to the protected preserves of academia. He belongs to everybody. Whalen's thorough survey of the authorship literature and his lucid analysis returns Shakespeare to the people. When Oxford prevails, lovers of Shakespeare everywhere, understanding better what he wrote and why, will experience a richer understanding of the poems and plays and, most important, of life itself. That's the priceless gift that Shakespeare has given us.

Ambassador Paul H. Nitze
Diplomat-in-residence at SAIS,
The Johns Hopkins Nitze School
Washington, D.C.

Preface

William Shakespeare is the only major literary figure whose personal identity is a matter of long-standing and continuing dispute. That he is also generally considered the greatest poet/ dramatist the world has ever known adds to the extraordinary nature of the controversy. To the casual reader it might seem incredible that doubts should still be raised about the very identity of so famous a literary figure. He flourished in London at the height of the Renaissance and at a time when Queen Elizabeth's England was emerging as the premier naval power of the world. His work was not hidden; his poems and plays were among the most successful of his time. Since then, his works and his biography have been the subject of the most intense scholarly study. Still, the doubts about his identity persist.

This book is intended for the general reader who would like to know why the controversy over his identity continues and what is known about the leading challenger for authorship honors. For those who enjoy probing a mystery, the literary works and historical records provide fascinating puzzles, intriguing clues, and provocative evidence. *Life* magazine once called it "history's biggest literary whodunnit."[1]

The life of no other literary figure has been so intensively researched, studied, and debated. The experts in the literary and historical records of Shakespeare's times have been sifting the evidence for almost two centuries. Their research reports, articles, monographs, and scholarly books now number in the thousands.

The reader can be assured, however, that evaluating the principal arguments in the controversy need not be feared as a formidable undertaking that requires years of study, special expertise, and familiarity with the academic jargon of English literature professors. Proficiency in literary exegesis is not required, nor is the ability to scrutinize Elizabethan manuscripts. The leading Shakespeareans have taken the scholarly research and produced biographies for general readers—biographies that reflect the conventional view in academia of who Shakespeare was and what kind of life he led. The focus of this book is on these biographies.

In the conventional view, Shakespeare was the son of a glove maker and one-time alderman of Stratford-on-Avon who went to London and became the great poet and dramatist. Dissenters, however, have challenged that view for two centuries. They have raised significant questions about his personal life story, noting that, for one of the most famous writers of his time, it was singularly devoid of literary content. They have expressed serious doubts whether he really was the poet/dramatist, and over the years they have proposed almost sixty candidates as the "true author" whose works appeared under the pseudonym William Shakespeare.

Over the years thousands of books and articles have been written on the Shakespeare authorship question. Among the more prominent literary figures who have expressed doubts about the conventional attribution are John Greenleaf Whittier, Ralph Waldo Emerson, Walt Whitman, Mark Twain, Henry James, John Galsworthy, Sigmund Freud, Maxwell Perkins, and Clifton Fadiman, who was awarded the National Book Foundation's 1993 Medal for Distinguished Contribution to American Letters. Several television programs have explored the issue, most notably the hour-long "Frontline" PBS-TV program broadcast in April 1989 and again in December 1992. In 1991 the *Atlantic Monthly* devoted its cover and five articles to the controversy. In recent years, the issue has even been debated in a moot court before three justices of the Supreme Court of the United States, in a second moot court before three senior jurists of Great Britain, and in a mock trial in November 1993 that was sponsored by the Boston Bar Association and the Shakespeare Oxford Society. In the twentieth century the field of some sixty candidates for authorship laurels was narrowed essentially to two—the incumbent from Stratford-on-Avon and the challenger, Edward de Vere, the seventeenth earl of Oxford. The challenger is relatively new to the scene. Many who have heard about the authorship controversy may be under the impression that it is based on a worn-out theory about Sir Francis Bacon or Christopher Marlowe. Oxford, however, has eclipsed all the other candidates, including Bacon, Marlowe, and the sixth earl of Derby, the three with the most widespread support in the nineteenth and early twentieth centuries. The evidence that has been developed for Oxford is far more persuasive. The Oxfordians, his supporters, maintain that it is even far more persuasive than the evidence for the incumbent from Stratford.

Edward de Vere, seventeenth earl of Oxford, was a cultured, controversial courtier in the court of Queen Elizabeth I, who shared Shakespeare's interest in literature and the theater. During his youth he was a ward of the Crown. His guardian, later to be his father-in-law, was William Cecil, Lord Burghley, the model for Polonius in *Hamlet*.

In his mid-twenties Oxford traveled on the Continent for more than a year, mainly in France and Italy, the setting for many of the plays. For much of his life he was associated with a group of writers and was a patron of acting companies. His own early poetry is quite Shakespearean, and his contemporaries praised him for his poetry and for his plays, although no plays attributed to his name have been found. His literary activities under his own name ceased about the time that the poems and plays of Shakespeare began to appear.

The works of Shakespeare mirror Oxford's life. In them can be found a surprising number of parallels and allusions to his education, marriage, travels, theater activities, and personal concerns. Some of them are specific and quite striking. *Hamlet*, in particular, reflects specific incidents in Oxford's life. Other plays do the same to a lesser extent, especially *All's Well That Ends*

Well, Romeo and Juliet, and *The Merchant of Venice.* For many who examine the case for Oxford, these parallels and allusions to his life are strong evidence that he was the writer behind the pseudonym William Shakespeare.

Scholars who maintain that Oxford was the author have also written articles and books for the general public. They have had more than seventy years to research Oxford's life and develop their case for his authorship. Despite a lack of support by universities and foundations, they have turned up a surprising amount of direct evidence for Oxford.

The time is right for the general reader to sit back and evaluate the evidence and conclusions presented by the experts. Academic scholars in the universities naturally would prefer that only accredited specialists, namely those in academia, be permitted to weigh the evidence. Scholars on both sides of the issue, however, have written for the general public. It seems reasonable, therefore, for the general reader to examine the arguments and counter-arguments and decide which are the more persuasive.

Any discussion of the authorship of Shakespeare's works requires making a distinction between the author, whoever he was, and the man from Stratford-on-Avon, whose authorship credentials are being questioned. Coherent discussion is impossible if they both have the same name. Clarity is obtained by referring to the Stratford man as Will Shakspere, the way his name was spelled in the Stratford church records. The author, whoever he was, is Shakespeare, the way the name appeared on the poems and plays. Thus, those who believe the man from Stratford wrote the works of Shakespeare are Stratfordians. Those who maintain that someone else was the author are non-Stratfordians or, more pointedly, anti-Stratfordians. Understandably, Stratfordians are not always happy with this distinction. They prefer to modernize, or regularize, the Stratford man's name to Shakespeare. To do so when discussing authorship issues, however, would make rational discussion almost impossible.

As an introduction to the Shakespeare authorship question, this book compares the arguments for and against Will Shakspere and Oxford. It analyzes the biography of Shakespeare as written for the general public by academic scholars who believe that he was Will Shakspere of Stratford-on-Avon. And it evaluates the case for Oxford as developed by the independent scholars, primarily J. Thomas Looney, Bernard M. Ward, Eva Turner Clark, Dorothy Ogburn and Charlton Ogburn, Sr., Charlton Ogburn, and Ruth Loyd Miller. The book therefore examines what are usually called secondary sources, that is, works of synthesis, commentary, and interpretation written for the lay person by expert scholars who have studied the primary sources. These primary sources include manuscripts and book editions, court records, letters, and other documents of the times.

Neither man left any records that directly claim authorship of Shakespeare's works. There are no manuscripts of the plays and poems, much less signed manuscripts. No documents openly identify either man as the author. No contemporary wrote a biography; in the seventeenth century there was no literary biography as such. No one attempted a biography until a century after both men were dead. Even then it was only a brief sketch. Lacking proof positive or the proverbial smoking gun, scholars rely on the accumulation of historical facts, contemporary testimony, and allusions in Shakespeare's works to build their biographies. Inevitably, some of it is inference and conjecture.

Since no single piece of evidence clinches the case for either man, the cumulative effect of the evidence for each is of paramount importance. In this book the accumulation of evidence, one piece after another, is analyzed to see wherein lies the preponderance of evidence. Just as in a trial by jury, where ordinary citizens render a verdict based on evidence and testimony presented by experts, the general reader can decide the merits in the case of the seventeenth earl of Oxford versus Will Shakspere of Stratford-on-Avon.

Obviously, my conclusion is that the authorship controversy is valid and that the preponderance of evidence supports the case for Oxford as the author. Otherwise, there would be no reason to write the book. Writers analyzing a controversy cannot wholly eliminate bias. No one can guarantee complete impartiality; that would be inhuman. Writers, however, can recognize the existence of bias, warn their readers about it, and then try to dampen its effects. My goal in setting out was to be even-handed, open, and impartial. The challenge was to be as objective as is humanly possible and to present the best possible case for each man, weighing the merits of each.

Some literary critics and scholars in the late twentieth century, even some readers of Shakespeare and performers of his plays, maintain that they have no interest in the author, whoever he was and whatever his life and times. For them, the works alone have validity for study. Presumably they also have no interest in the life and times of Leo Tolstoy, Charles Dickens, Jane Austen, Marcel Proust, Mark Twain, Emily Dickinson, or any other creative artist. For them literary biography is worthless. This book is not for them, although there is always the hope they may change their mind.

Not infrequently someone apprised of the Shakespeare authorship question asks why anyone should want to spend time on it. Several reasons may be offered. First, it is a fascinating literary detective story for anyone interested in Shakespeare and how writers create great literature. Second, it concerns the most influential dramatic poetry ever written; if perchance Oxford was the man behind the pseudonym Shakespeare, simple justice requires that he receive the recognition that is his due. Third, it offers the prospect of whole new worlds of discovery for Shakespearean scholars. Finally, and most important of all, it could lead to an enormously enhanced appreciation of the poems and plays for general readers and theatergoers. If Oxford is seen as the author, the plays and poems take on entirely new and rewarding dimensions. For example, many of the famous problems in the "problem plays" evaporate.

This book will have served its purpose if it leads the reader to compare the orthodox biographies of conventional scholarship with the works of independent Oxfordian scholars, such as Looney, Ogburn, and Miller. Even better, if college students and graduate students in English literature and Elizabethan history use it as a springboard to question the conventional belief in Will Shakspere of Stratford-on-Avon as the author. Best of all, if it leads the general reader to a new and broader appreciation of Shakespeare's works, which might well have been the works of an Elizabethan nobleman, poet, dramatist, and patron of acting companies, a man who seems to have possessed outstanding qualifications as the true author of the poems and plays of William Shakespeare.

The notes for each chapter provide citations, additional information, sidelights, and curious facts for readers who want to go beyond the book's main narrative argument. Citations of other books and records could easily have been multiplied by ten. They have been given for facts, claims, and arguments that seemed especially pertinent or controversial, or perhaps hard to locate. The citations are not always to original sources of a discovery or insight, but to the most convenient, authoritative sources for the general reader. Many books and articles of original scholarship are out of print and not in most municipal libraries. No slight is intended, and apologies are offered if original scholarship is not sufficiently credited.

Acknowledgement is due all those who allowed me to test my analysis against their knowledge. My greatest debt is to Charlton Ogburn, whose landmark book, *The Mysterious William Shakespeare: The Myth and the Reality*, is the most comprehensive and authoritative presentation of the case against Will Shakspere and for the earl of Oxford. He has been a most generous and most unsparing critic. Ruth Loyd Miller also provided extensive comments that resulted in significant improvements. The resources of the Harvard College Library, with its extensive collection of works Stratfordian and Oxfordian, have been invaluable and are gratefully acknowledged.

Manuscript reviews and valuable assistance were also provided by Charles Vere, Lord Burford; Gerald E. Downs; Gary B. Goldstein; E. J. Kahn, Jr.; Felicia Londré; Richard Lovelace; and Roger Stritmatter. Their corrections and suggestions for improvements were perceptive and most beneficial. As must always be the case, however, any errors in fact and flaws in interpretation that remain must be charged to the author's account.

Part One

THE INCUMBENT: THE MAN FROM STRATFORD

Chapter One

A Strikingly Mundane Life

A difficult dilemma confronts biographers who tell the story of the glove maker's son from Stratford-on-Avon who is supposed to have become the world's greatest poet and dramatist.[1] On the one hand, scholars over the centuries have turned up a fair amount of historical information about his life in business and real estate and, to a much lesser extent, as an actor or theater personage. On the other hand, none of the information from his lifetime has anything to do with the writing of plays and poems. Only years after his death was there any testimony that he was the author of the plays of Shakespeare. But the testimony was not only posthumous, it was ambiguous.

His biographers, obliged to construct some sort of meaningful account of his life for their books and introductions to the plays, display a wide range of views about the available evidence. Some find it utterly useless; others find it perfectly adequate. Some find a mystery; some no mystery at all. A few of them struggle with the biographical tradition they have inherited. Their biographies, however, end up leaving the reader puzzled about how much is known and what to make of it. A survey of their views is illuminating.[2]

The opening sentence of *A Companion to Shakespeare Studies* reads: "Of the life of Shakespeare little is known."

In more elaborate terms, George Saintsbury, the eminent literary critic, concluded: "The results of the most ferocious industry spent upon unearthing and analyzing every date and detail of Shakespeare's life are on the whole very meager, and for literary purposes almost entirely unimportant, while with guesswork we will have nothing to do."

Similarly, the *Concise Cambridge History of English Literature* condemns most of the great quantity of dates and details that have been unearthed as "utterly useless and irrelevant."

E. K. Chambers, one of the most renowned Shakespearean scholars of all time, gave his two-volume, biographical opus the provocative subtitle, *A Study of Facts and Problems*. The problems greatly outweighed the facts, which support a biographical narrative of only ninety-one pages, less than ten percent of the two volumes. The rest is documents and commentary.

Sixty years after Chambers, Professor Terry Eagleton was of the same mind. He ends a book review that is critical of an overly imaginative biography with these words: "There is no mystery to the man Shakespeare, no secret life, no elusive depth. It is just that we happen to know almost nothing about him, which is quite a different matter."

Giles E. Dawson, emeritus curator at the Folger Shakespeare Library, agrees and adds: "In this kind of biographical obscurity Shakespeare is like all other Elizabethan dramatists and, for that matter, nearly all of his contemporaries."

Dawson's colleagues at the Folger, however, do find this obscurity somewhat mysterious. The editors of the Folger editions of the plays include a brief biography asserting that documents tie him "inextricably" to Shakespeare's works. Not a single document is cited, however, and the editors must conclude: "How this particular man produced the works that dominate the culture of much of the world almost four hundred years after his death is one of life's mysteries."

At Harvard there are no mysteries. In the prestigious Riverside edition of Shakespeare, Professor Harry Levin of Harvard opens the biographical section with the assertion:

Contrary to a fairly widespread impression, there is no special mystery about his life. Indeed, it is unusually well documented for a commoner's of his period....But these details [including more than a hundred documents and fifty literary allusions], even when they have been eked out by traditions and conjectures, scarcely combine to portray a vivid personality.

Levin's conclusion: "His existence would not seem uneventful if we consider that the main events were the thirty-eight plays." Levin's predecessor, George Lyman Kittredge, did acknowledge some puzzlement. In an address on the three hundredth anniversary of Shakespeare's death he said, "Of Shakspere's [sic] life we know a good deal, but nothing that explains him." And later, "Still, I can analyze Shakspere roughly, though I cannot account for him." And again, "Unquestionably, the man is there; the real Shakspere is somehow latent in his plays; but how is one to extract him?" Kittredge had no answer.

Bolder by far is Professor Stanley Wells. In his introduction to the Oxford edition of Shakespeare he asserts: "We know more about him than about any other dramatist of his times except Ben Jonson." But he cites only two pieces of evidence linking him to the poems and plays, neither of them from his lifetime. The main biographical facts are business dealings.

Equally confident is Professor A. L. Rowse, a prolific Shakespeare biographer, who writes in *Shakespeare: the Man* that "we know more about him than about any other dramatist of the time, with the exception of Ben Jonson." The same opinion, in almost the same words, is expressed by Marchette Chute in *Shakespeare of London* probably the most popular biography of the late twentieth century, and by Sylvan Barnet in his introduction to the Signet editions of the plays.

Professor S. Schoenbaum is more restrained. He laments the lack of

memorabilia expressive of authorial personality: no letters, no conversations; it goes without saying, no diaries. Those records we do have mostly betoken formal, often legal occasions: register entries, deeds of purchase, court notices, a last will and testament, and the like. Yet for Shakespeare more records have survived than for most Elizabethan dramatists, and these are not without interest or significance.

Professor David Bevington is somewhat more satisfied with the record. In his introduction to the complete works, he states: "What we know of Shakespeare's life so far [i.e., to age twenty-nine] is really quite considerable....Though lacking in the personal details we would like to have, it is both adequate and plausible." A biography that is adequate and plausible but without personal details for half a man's life span hardly inspires much confidence.

The *Encyclopedia Britannica* recognizes the problem. Its article begins, "Although the amount of factual knowledge available about Shakespeare is surprisingly large for one of his station in life, many find it a little disappointing."

Disappointed biographers often resort to conjecture and speculation. "The facts in this case are few and far between, and require a great deal of conjecture," observes Norrie Epstein in *The Friendly Shakespeare.* Her chapter titled "Some Biographical Bones" pointedly recalls Mark Twain's jibe that Shakespeare's biography, like a museum dinosaur, consists of a few bones and lots of plaster.

So also with the *Cambridge Guide to Literature in English* which opens its Shakespeare section with these words: "In a flamboyant age and a notoriously flamboyant profession—he was an active member of a theater company for at least twenty years—Shakespeare was notably reticent. As a result, scholars have had painstakingly to piece together the story of his life from surviving scraps of evidence, and there remains ample room for speculation."

Inference is also the methodology of Professor G. B. Harrison. In his edition of the major plays he calls the biographical facts "commonplace," and he can only conclude that "literary persons, even the greatest, are seldom spectacular." He then moves on to inferences from the plays and poems: Shakespeare must have been a soldier; he must have gone to sea; he must have lived a full life. Harrison, however, can find nothing in the historical records of the man to support such inferences.[3]

The range of scholarly opinion in this long list of citations from eminent Shakespeareans is dismaying: almost nothing is known about him...we know more about him than almost any other dramatist...the facts are a little disappointing...what is known is utterly useless...what is known is surprisingly large...there's a mystery...there's no special mystery...there's ample room for speculation. These contradictory assertions, all taken from standard works, must leave the general reader in a quandary, wondering whom to believe.

The contradictions can, in fact, be reconciled, but only when a very significant distinction is made. The distinction can be simply stated: On the one hand, scholars have discovered a great deal about the life of Will Shakspere of Stratford-on-Avon. On the other hand, nothing in his life has anything to do with anything literary. The scholar who says that almost nothing is known about him is looking for his life as a writer, but finds almost nothing. The scholar who says that what's known is surprising large has fastened on the numerous records of his money-lending, real estate business, and theater investments. Those who are balked in their attempts to reconcile the mundane man and his literary reputation call it a mystery; and the temptation to solve the mystery with speculation is hard to resist.

Ralph Waldo Emerson recognized in 1850 the difficulty of reconciling the life of the Stratford man and the works of the poet/dramatist. Citing the judgment that Shakespeare "was a jovial actor and manager," Emerson said, "I cannot marry this fact to his verse. Other admirable men have led lives in some sort of keeping with their thought; but this man, in wide contrast."[4]

The dilemma of so much research yielding nothing literary about the man himself during his lifetime has led many to question whether he was indeed the author of the works of Shakespeare. The questioning took hold in earnest in the mid-nineteenth century, when Emerson and others pondered the dilemma. The doubters quickly seized upon Sir Francis Bacon, the erudite philosopher, essayist, and statesman, as the supposed author. Over the decades, other candidates were put forward. In all, about sixty have been nominated by those convinced that the magnificent works of Shakespeare could not have been written by the glover's son from Stratford-on-Avon who was known there as Will Shakspere—the most common spelling of his name, with variants, from his birth to his death. The doubting and dissenting has continued throughout the twentieth century. Those who have doubted or rejected altogether the belief that Will Shakspere of Stratford-on-Avon was the author give four main reasons. First, the documents from his lifetime describe him only as a businessman and real estate investor, with some minor connection to the theater—but not as a playwright. Second, evidence that one would expect from the lifetime of a poet and playwright is totally lacking; that testimony did not come until years after he died and the circumstances of it are suspect. Third, the records of his lifetime almost always spelled his name Shakspere, or some variant, while the name on the plays and poems was almost always spelled Shakespeare, about half the time with a hyphen, which generally denoted a made-up name or pseudonym. Finally, Will Shakspere's mundane life record does not square with the depth of classical education, the keen knowledge of France and Italy, the rich life experience, and the aristocratic attitude that are all expressed so powerfully in the works of Shakespeare.

For the first thirty years of his life, all that is known about Will Shakspere is found in the records of his baptism, his marriage, and the baptisms of his children, plus a passing mention in a lawsuit brought by his father over property. Nothing else for the first thirty years, the most formative years of an artist's life.

He was baptized William, son of John Shakspere, on April 26, 1564, in Stratford-on-Avon. His biographers like to assume that his birthday was three days earlier, April 23, because that is the day on which he died fifty-two years later. It also happens to be the feast day of St. George, the patron saint of England. His father, John Shakspere, was a leather worker and glove maker and for a time was alderman of Stratford. John Shakspere signed his name with a mark, as did several other town officials. Scholars generally conclude that he was probably illiterate, not unusual at that time and in a town of fifteen hundred people, a four-day journey from London.[5]

After Will Shakspere's birth, the next record is his marriage license. He was eighteen years old; Anne Hathaway was twenty-six and pregnant. The record, actually a dispensation from banns, spelled his name Shaxpere and Shagspere. A daughter, Susanna, was baptized six months later, and less than two years after that twins were baptized, a son and a daughter. The boy died at age eleven. The two daughters survived their father.

What Will Shakspere was doing as a boy, or adolescent, or young man in his twenties is not known. Nothing has been found. No Stratford school records for those years have been found. Biographers generally resort to conjecture and extrapolation, writing that he "undoubtedly" went to school, "probably" moved to London after the twins were born, and "must have become" an actor and dramatist there in his twenties. But there are no historical records or literary works that support, or contradict, such speculations. The record is a blank.[6]

When he was in his early thirties Will Shakspere's name began to turn up in the records. It appeared in some two dozen business and legal records spanning the next twenty years to his death in 1616. When he was twenty-eight he loaned money to a Londoner and went to court seven years later to collect it. When he was thirty-three he was already rich enough to buy the second-largest house in Stratford. The source of his early prosperity is difficult to document. Acting and playwriting paid very little, and he was not yet a partner in the theaters.

The year he turned thirty-four is unusual for its contrasts. For the first time, a poet/dramatist named Shakespeare, whoever he was, was praised in print as a sonneteer and as a playwright who was among the best for tragedy and comedy. The same name appeared that year (1598) on the title page of *Love's Labour's Lost*, the first of the plays to carry the author's name. Six other plays by Shakespeare had been printed earlier, but without any byline identifying the author.

In the same year, however, the legal records concerning Will Shakspere paint a contrasting picture. The records show that Will Shakspere of Stratford-on-Avon was involved in "a matter of tithes," was cited among others for hoarding grain during a famine, and was paid for a load of stone—all in Stratford. In

London, he was cited, for the second time, as a tax evader who could not be located. Improbably, the tax man could not locate the newly famous author, if he was the author.

Other records from Will Shakspere's thirties and forties are equally mundane. A Londoner seeks guarantees of personal safety from Shakspare, as it was spelled, and three others, including a theater owner. He again is delinquent in paying taxes. He buys more real estate in Stratford. He sues for small sums of money owed to him. He purchases a share of tithes, the rental income from farm land. He is involved in a dispute over land enclosures. He makes his will, which has nothing literary in it, and is buried under a gravestone that does not even carry his name.

In contrast to the extensive records of his business life and legal affairs, the lifetime records of his theater involvement are sparse and scattered.[7] They are barely sufficient to turn a businessman into a theater personage. None calls him a playwright. None of them are theater records. Four are government records that merely list him as a member of an acting company, and one of them is suspect. Two others are literary allusions subject to varying interpretations. Two more are in wills. One is a joke. (See appendix A.)

Only one of the records is interpreted by Stratfordian scholars as testimony that he was both an actor and a playwright. This is a complex literary allusion in *Greenes Groatsworth of Wit*. The Stratfordian interpretation of the allusive passage, which almost defies explication, is hotly contested by non-Stratfordians, who allege willful misreading. (Appendix B gives the text of the *Groatsworth* passage, which is discussed in chapter 4.)

Will Shakspere is widely taken to have been an actor on the Elizabethan stage, but the general reader will look in vain for details about his acting career. No records give him any role in any play, not even in the plays he is supposed to have written. Nothing suggests that he was performing regularly. Scholarly researchers have combed the theater records of the time, both in London and in the countryside where the acting companies toured, but Shakespeare's name, whatever the spelling, is nowhere to be found as an actor during his lifetime. The missing evidence makes it difficult to accept the traditional belief that Will Shakspere learned to write plays by performing as an actor on stage.

Only after Will Shakspere died was the name Shakespeare included in a list of cast members in specific plays, and then only three times. In the year of Will Shakspere's death (1616), Ben Jonson published his own works and put Shakespeare's name in the casts of two of his own plays that had been performed years before. Shakespeare's name led one of the cast lists.

This retroactive positioning by Ben Jonson of Shakespeare's name at the head of a list of actors in Jonson's plays is peculiar. At no time during Will Shakspere's lifetime had he been so recognized. His name in any of the spellings never appeared anywhere in theater records about actors.

Seven years later, Shakespeare's name again led a list of actors. The list was included in the first edition of his collected plays, the posthumous *First Folio*. Ben Jonson undoubtedly had a controlling hand in the prefatory materials in the *First Folio*, including the list of actors. Thus Ben Jonson was closely involved in the only three times that Shakespeare's name appeared as an actor in theatrical records. The validity of Jonson's testimony, particularly in the *First Folio*, thus becomes of crucial importance.

Will Shakspere's three-page, detailed will, written by an attorney, is the longest, most specific, and most personal legal record from his lifetime, but it is the will of a businessman. One of his two daughters, not his wife, was named as the principal beneficiary, and various complex contingencies for her offspring were spelled out. Several bequests were very specific, among them a silver bowl to his other daughter and, in an afterthought, his second-best bed to his wife.

Various sums of money were left to relatives and friends. One bequest was small sums for three theater associates for memorial rings, although without any words of praise or affection. This bequest, absent in the first, full draft, was also a late addition squeezed into the will between the lines.

The three signatures, one on each page, are in a labored and crabbed hand, nothing like what would be expected of a writer. Possibly he was gravely ill, perhaps with a stroke, as some Stratfordians suggest. Even so, the signature on the last page of the will, although quite competent, does not seem to reflect the hand of a man who penned almost a million words.

Will Shakspere was buried in Trinity Church at Stratford-on-Avon under a stone slab that did not even carry his name. That it is indeed his grave is inferred; stone slabs on either side of it carry the names of his wife and other family members. The only writing on the gravestone was a crude verse that has nothing to do with anything literary:

> Good friend for Jesus sake forebear,
> To dig the dust enclosed here:
> Blest be the man that spares these stones,
> And curst be he that moves my bones.

Biographers differ on whether Will Shakspere wrote the verse, but they believe it was intended to dissuade future church wardens from removing his remains to a charnel house to make room for more graves in the church.

Sometime during the next seven years a monument with a half-length bust was erected on the wall of the church. Early engravings of it depict a man with a drooping moustache leaning on what looks like a sack of wool or grain. In the intervening years someone changed the effigy. Today it depicts a man with a quill pen and sheet of paper leaning on what is clearly a pillow; and the drooping moustache has become an upturned moustache. The epitaph on the monument is more significant for what it doesn't say than for what it does.

Stratfordian scholars have no little difficulty reconciling this dull life with the towering genius and stupendous erudition shining forth from the works of Shakespeare. The renowned Professor Schoenbaum laments the unlikelihood that anyone will ever be able to write a satisfactory narrative biography. On the last page of *Shakespeare's Lives* he draws a melancholy conclusion: "Perhaps we should despair of ever bridging the vertiginous expanse between the sublimity of the subject and the mundane inconsequence of the documentary record."[8]

A sentence worth pondering. Here is one of the foremost Shakespearean scholars, a lifelong, staunch defender of the Stratfordian faith, concluding a 568-page study of the many biographies of Shakespeare with such a lament.

Schoenbaum's reluctant despair vividly illustrates the difficult dilemma facing traditional scholarship: How to reconcile the dull documentary record of his distinctly nonliterary life with the stunning accomplishments of the world's greatest poet and playwright. The leading scholars find it difficult, if not impossible, to effect a reconciliation. The general reader who looks at just two or three of the standard biographies of Shakespeare, with their liberal use of locutions such as "probably" and "must have," and with their dependence on inference and speculation to flesh out a portrait, will almost certainly conclude that there is, indeed, an authorship question worth studying.

If the complete and unadorned facts of Will Shakspere's life add up to "mundane inconsequence" for an academic scholar of the first rank, what is missing from Will Shakspere's life is even more surprising if he is supposed to be the successful poet and dramatist of London at the height of the English Renaissance.

Chapter Two

The Missing Literary Evidence

A tremendous silence marked the death of Will Shakspere of Stratford-on-Avon.

The gravestone in his own church did not even carry his name. Not a single eulogy has been found, although eulogies were common. Nobody mentioned his death in any writings at the time or for years afterwards, not even Ben Jonson, who remained silent for seven years before suddenly praising Shakespeare as "the soul of the age." In the year Will Shakspere died (1616), Ben Jonson published not a word about his death, although in the same year he did address poems to Philip Sidney, Francis Beaumont, and John Donne. Nothing was left by anyone in the court of King James I, who had supported an acting company that performed Shakespeare's plays regularly.

In Stratford, nothing from Will Shakspere's friends and neighbors where he was one of the richest landowners and should have been its most celebrated citizen, supposedly the successful poet and playwright in London and a familiar of the royal court. Nothing from his daughters, granted that they are generally believed to have been illiterate. Nothing from any of his descendants, ever.

Nothing, moreover, from his son-in-law, John Hall, a university graduate and physician whose wife inherited most of Will Shakspere's estate. Dr. Hall kept medical diaries in Latin and referred to one patient, Michael Drayton, as "an excellent poet."[1] But he left not a word about his father-in-law, Will Shakspere. Nothing at the time from Drayton, either, although he was a prolific poet and London playwright. Finally, not a word from anyone in Stratford in the generations that followed, not from Will's supposed schoolmasters, his friends, or his family, who might have taken pride, if they thought they could, in his considerable success in the popular theaters and at court.

The silence surrounding the death of Will Shakspere appears to go beyond indifference and almost amount to a rejection of the idea that he was anyone of any literary consequence. The silence stands in stark contrast to the encomiums delivered upon the deaths of other writers and theater figures. For example, Francis Beaumont, a playwright who had died just a month before, drew an outpouring of eulogies, and was buried in Westminster Abbey. The deaths of Edmund Spenser and Ben Jonson were similarly recognized, and they, too, received the honor of burial in Westminster Abbey. Even Richard Burbage, the actor, was accorded eulogies at his death. At Will Shakspere's death, as in his life, notice of literary achievement, if any existed, was missing.

Although the man known to his family, friends, and neighbors as Will Shakspere of Stratford-on-Avon has been almost universally accepted as the world's greatest poet/dramatist, there is nothing literary in the records of his lifetime. Armies of scholars have sifted and scrutinized thousands of documents, but to no avail. They have turned up only the legal, real estate, commercial, and government records of a businessman, possibly a bit-part actor, with some theater connections. During his lifetime, Will Shakspere is nowhere on record as a writer. Only if the poet/dramatist's byline, spelled Shakespeare, is bestowed on him does he become the supposed author. That bestowal was only made after his death, and then in vague and ambiguous terms that render it suspect.

Nothing has been found that would suggest that Will Shakspere wrote anything at all, much less the world's greatest poems and plays. No notes, no journals, no early drafts, no letters, even though his house stayed in the family for two generations after he died.[2] Nothing in his detailed will about the eighteen plays that had yet to be printed when he died. That no manuscripts have been found is not all that unusual for Elizabethan times; they belonged to the acting companies or printers, who disposed of them. But no one has been able to find anything written by the hand of Will Shakspere, supposedly the well-known and successful poet and playwright of Stratford and London.

There is no evidence that he had any library. No mention of books in his will, even though it was very detailed and disposed specifically of other household items. His sword was left to a friend, a silver bowl to one of his daughters, the silver plate to his granddaughter, his clothes to his sister, and his second-best bed to his wife. Other men of his time mentioned books in their wills. Not Will Shakspere. None of his heirs left any word about any books in the house they inherited. No book of his, if he had any, has turned up in libraries in other houses where they might have found their way after his death.

Not a scrap of writing in his hand has survived.[3] Six signatures, all on legal documents and all from the last four years of his life, are spelled out in a crabbed hand.[4] They look like a child's attempt to copy a signature. The smooth flourish of a signature, whether legible or illegible, that would be expected of a writer who had penned nearly a million words, is missing. Handwriting experts differ on whether the crabbed signatures are all by the same hand. The three on his will are questioned by the document's custodian in London, who maintains that it was usual in those days for a clerk to sign for someone making a will.[5]

The records of Will Shakspere's life and family have been exhaustively researched by scholars searching for something, anything, literary. What they have found is far from what would be expected for an ambitious, prolific, and successful dramatist. What they hoped to find is missing.

Even more striking is the total lack of any references during his lifetime to Will Shakspere of Stratford as an author in any letters, notes, essays, diaries, or any written communication by his friends, relatives, neighbors, colleagues, or critics, whether in London or Stratford. The record is silent. There are many contemporary references to Shakespeare the author, the name on the well-regarded plays and poems, but not one of them ever links

Belott-Mountjoy Affidavit, 1612.   Public Records Office.

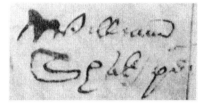

Blackfriars Conveyance, 1613. Guildhall
Library

Blackfriars Mortgage, 1613. British Library.

From the three pages of the will.   Public Records Office.
25 March 1616.

The six purported signatures of Will Shakspere. The three at the bottom, from his will, are thought to be shaky because of terminal illness; one has deteriorated over time. In the bottom signature, "By me William" is in a different and more proficient hand than "Shak-spere" that follows. The three signatures at the top were written three to four years earlier. None spells it Shakespeare. (By permission of the Shakespeare Oxford Society.)

the author to Will Shakspere of Stratford, or, indeed, to any identifiable person who was alive at the time of the reference. It is
as if no one knew who the author was, or as if no one would
acknowledge knowing who he was.

Conventional biographers have to account for the fact that Will
Shakspere, if he was the author, seems to have deliberately
shunned the literary spotlight. Generally, they conclude that he
knew playwriting was considered low-class and that he was
more interested in his reputation as a businessman. The records
of the time do describe him as a successful moneylender, grain
dealer, and investor in real estate and theaters. In his biography,
Dennis Kay explains it this way: "He seems to have been much
more concerned to consolidate his business interests and preserve his estates in Stratford than to prepare his works for publication that would enable him to speak to posterity." Historian
A. L. Rowse writes: "Shakespeare's ego was satisfied by recognition as a gentleman and poet; his being an actor and writing
plays came somewhat lower in his scale of values." Russell Fraser, another biographer, says simply: "Shakespeare, self-effacing,
kept his head down."[6]

Will Shakspere was curiously silent during all the momentous
events of his lifetime. For example, when Queen Elizabeth died
and James I was crowned king in 1603, thirteen years before Will
Shakspere's death, poems and commentary poured from the
pens of London's literary luminaries. Nothing, however, from
Will Shakspere, although that was the year *Hamlet* was published. Unaccountably, his voice was missing.

Will Shakspere is supposed to have been an actor who soaked
up the craft and art of playwriting from the stage. If so, the
record is remarkably skimpy. The name Shakespeare appears
only half a dozen times as a player or member of an acting company, but not one of them describes any role in a play or any
recognition he might have received for whatever acting talent he
may have had. One would expect to find his name in one of the
cast lists telling which actors played which parts. Nowhere has
his name been found in the records of his lifetime, not even as
an actor in the plays he is supposed to have written. Only in the
year of his death did his name appear in a list of actors who
performed in a play, and that was in the publication of two plays

by Ben Jonson that had been performed years earlier; and Jonson's motives for belatedly including Shakespeare's name in the list can be questioned.

Millions of tourists have gazed up at the monument on the wall of Trinity Church in Stratford-on-Avon. It seems to be an authentic memorial to Shakespeare the poet/dramatist. Upon closer examination, however, the effigy and the inscription are not what they seem to be.

The inscription on the monument, which was probably erected sometime in the seven years between Will Shakspere's death and publication of the *First Folio*, is not what might be expected if it were intended to pay tribute to one of the better known poets and dramatists of the times. His full name does not appear, only Shakspeare, which is a Stratford variant spelling and not that of the famous author of London. Without a first name, it does not distinguish the deceased from the many other Shaksperes in the parish. The name is buried in the middle of the cryptic, eight-line epitaph.

The text of the epitaph is banal and even contradictory. Most significant, nowhere are the plays or poems mentioned. No quotation from Shakespeare is used, nor is Will Shakspere praised as the author of them. Any word of tribute to a renowned dramatist is missing, as is any word about the theater or acting.

Whoever composed the epitaph exhorts passersby to slow down and "read if you can" (a bizarre exhortation) who was placed within the monument on the wall; but Will Shakspere's body was placed under the tombstone in the church floor. The remaining three lines refer to "quick nature" having died with him, since all he has written "leaves living art, but page, to serve his wit."[7] Certainly not high praise, and not a word about poetry or plays or the theater. It is difficult to escape the conclusion that the epitaph writer could not or would not write a proper tribute to the famous poet/dramatist.

The effigy itself is of doubtful authenticity. In today's monument it is a half-length bust of a man with an upturned moustache and goatee. He holds a large quill pen in one hand and a sheet of paper in the other. For some reason, both hands rest on what quite clearly represents a pillow. This effigy, however, is almost certainly not what was originally erected in the church.

An early engraving of it shows a man with a drooping moustache clutching what appears to be a sack of wool or grain, and Will Shakspere was a grain dealer. There is no pen or paper in the engraving, which was published forty years after his death and again seventy-five years later. A similar engraving was used by the first Shakespeare editor and biographer, Nicholas Rowe, in his 1709 edition of the plays, and it was still without pen or paper.

The transformation of the effigy from grain dealer to writer apparently occurred a century or more after Will Shakspere's death. In the 1700s and again in the mid-1800s the bust was reportedly repaired and "beautified." Today the effigy, equipped with pen and paper and preparing to write on a pillow, gazes out over the heads of visitors to the church. That is probably not, however, the effigy that Will Shakspere's survivors and friends saw as a memorial to him.[8]

Will Shakspere's life record being devoid of anything literary, it's not surprising that the way the plays and the *Sonnets* were published presents problems for biographers who believe that he was the author.

A major problem is that the author himself is missing from the publication of his works. Half of the plays of Shakespeare were published one by one in quarto format while Will Shakspere was alive. Yet there is no evidence that he took any interest in their publication. Some of the plays came out in different quarto versions, and scholars to this day debate whether one of the quartos or the *First Folio* version is more authentic.[9] Will Shakspere, presumably the self-taught, ambitious playwright, didn't seem to care. Nothing has been found to indicate his preference. Nearly all the quarto editions are considered to have been pirated editions; again, nothing has been found to indicate that Will Shakspere, if he was the author, cared.

Other playwrights did move on occasion to protect their works and see to their proper publication. Ben Jonson edited and published his *Works*. Will Shakspere did not. Nor are there records that he was paid for any of the plays, even though playwriting and acting are supposed to have been his main sources of income. Others were paid.

No single item of missing evidence of authorship is crucial to

The earliest illustration of the "Shakspeare" monument in Trinity Church, Stratford-on-Avon, from Dugdale's *Antiquities of Warwickshire* (1656). A half-century later Nicholas Rowe used a similar engraving of a man with a drooping moustache holding a sack of wool or grain (and still no pen or paper) to illustrate his edition of Shakespeare. Two decades after that, the Dugdale engraving was reprinted unchanged in a second edition of Dugdale's book. (By permission of the Folger Shakespeare Library.)

The "Shakspeare" monument in Trinity Church, Stratford-on-Avon. The effigy now has an upturned moustache and a goatee; pen and paper appear in his hands, which rest on a pillow. (By permission of the Folger Shakespeare Library.)

the case against Will Shakspere as the author. Each can be explained away as insignificant, or a mistake, or the result of poor record-keeping, or one of Will Shakspere's idiosyncracies, or simply as not untypical of the times. But taken together, their cumulative effect is powerful. To the end of his days Will Shakspere of Stratford-on-Avon never claimed to be the author of Shakespeare's poems and plays. Nor does any record survive suggesting he took any interest in the publication of the plays. Even after his death, the inscription on his monument failed to attribute the published poems and plays to him.

THE MISSING APPRENTICESHIP

Stratfordian chronology puts the writing of the early plays and poetry at a time when Will Shakspere was still in his mid-twenties, just three years after the twins were born in Stratford. According to the *Riverside Shakespeare*, the first plays were begun when he was about twenty-four years old. In the next five years or so, he is supposed to have written as many as twelve major works, all of which show a wide-ranging experience of life and a profound knowledge of the classics, English history, and the ways of the nobility. The dozen works were five history plays, including *Richard III*; four comedies, including *Love's Labour's Lost*; the tragedy *Titus Andronicus*; and the two long narrative poems, plus some of the sonnets. Rarely is there mention of how new he was to London or how he was able to learn about aristocratic and royal lifestyles without leaving a trace.

If Will Shakspere was the author, his initial learning curve was not just steep, it was vertical. The earliest plays and poems are fully realized. Some of them are even more polished than plays that scholars date years later. But missing from the early twenties of this supposed poet/dramatist is any evidence of any apprenticeship.

The only explanation that can be offered for this precocius maturity of artistry and in-depth knowledge of aristocratic life at such an early age is "superhuman genius" or "divine inspiration." Non-Stratfordians, however, find it beyond belief that genius or miraculous intervention could explain the sophisticated experience of life, the classical education, the richness of vocabulary, and the maturity of expression shown in the early works of Shakespeare. They have looked for other explanations, that is, for another author.

But that is only the beginning of Will Shakespere's phenomenal accomplishments in his early twenties, if he was the author. He was also very busy. He is presumed to have left Stratford sometime after the twins were born in February 1585, perhaps that year or the next, when he was twenty-two years old. If he joined an acting company right away to make a living and learn the trade, he would have had little time for anything else. The acting companies staged about fifty different plays a year. Rarely was the same play performed on succeeding days; there were no "long runs." Acting troupes were not large. Everyone must have performed in almost every play, often taking more than one role. The actors had to learn dozens of different parts. From what can be determined from theater records, an actor typically would perform in one play during an afternoon, then learn a new part or parts, run through the new play in rehearsal and act in it the next day.[10]

At the same time, Will Shakspere, if the author, was presumably educating himself in English history and the Latin classics; learning two modern languages; acquiring accurate, detailed lore about warfare, law, botany, medicine, falconry, bowling, and many other aristocratic activities; and gaining a close familiarity with the ways of royalty, court life, and military command. On top of all this he was running his real estate and grain business in Stratford, a four-day journey from London, where his wife and three children apparently stayed. All this without a public library, electric lights, buses, a word processor, or a fax machine.

Adding to his many challenges in his early twenties would have been the burden of his Warwickshire dialect and accent, which were probably barely understandable in London. He would have had to shed his accent quickly to succeed on the stage in major roles, if he had any. To write the plays and poems, he would have had to replace the vocabulary and syntax of the Warwickshire dialect with the highly sophisticated and rapidly evolving English of literary London. Both feats of linguistic and cultural transformation seem beyond belief, even for a superhuman genius. He would have had to accomplish them in just three or four years at the most, between the birth of the twins, when he was twenty-one, and his first plays when he was about twenty-four by conventional chronology. For some non-Stratfordians, the burden of his Warwickshire dialect and accent alone preclude his being the author of the works of Shake-speare.[11]

THE MISSING AUTHOR OF THE *SONNETS*

The author is also missing from the publication of *Shake-speares Sonnets.* The 154 sonnets were published under circumstances that raise several questions about whether Will Shakspere of Stratford-on-Avon really was the author.[12] The sonnets themselves are full of misprints and mistakes, indicating that the author did no proofreading. The dedication was written, not by the author, but by the printer. Scholars conclude that the printing was an unauthorized piracy. In contrast, fifteen years earlier *Venus and Adonis* and *The Rape of Lucrece,* the two, long narrative poems, had carried dedications by "William Shakespeare" and were clear of errors. Not the *Sonnets.* The author was missing.

If Will Shakspere was the author, he should have been able to ensure that his most intimate poetry, his only poetry written in the first person singular, was printed correctly, if he wanted it printed at all. Nothing in the record gives any cause for doubt that he could have tried either to prevent piracy or supervise proofing and publication. He was forty-five years old and still active. Records for the year of publication (1609) have him filing suit for a debt of six pounds, and pursuing it. The following year he was involved in legal action over real estate. And he had seven more years to live.

The title page, however, reads as if the author were dead. The title itself, *Shake-speares Sonnets,* is a locution usually reserved for the works of an author who is dead. But Will Shakspere was still among the living when the book was published. For a living author the publisher would have used the byline "By William Shake-speare." (Oxfordians note that the seventeenth earl of Oxford, whom they maintain to have been the author of the *Sonnets,* had been dead five years at the time they were published.)

Once the author's name was put in the book's title, there was no reason to use a byline. That would have been redundant. But the space for it was there on the title page. In many books of the time the space for the author's byline was between two horizontal lines on the bottom half of the title page. In *Shake-speares Sonnets* the horizontal lines are there but for no obvious reason, because the space between them was left blank, as if to signal that the author was missing.[13]

The dedication of the *Sonnets*, written by the printer, was addressed to a Mr. W. H., whose identity has been much disputed. The text of the dedication, a cryptic construction of twenty-six words, mentions "our ever-living poet," as if the author, again, were no longer among the living. "Ever-living," then and now, refers to someone who has died but lives on in memory or in his works. To refer to Will Shakspere as ever-living would not have made sense. He was still very much alive.

If the *Sonnets* had appeared with only one or two of these problems, there would be little reason to raise questions about their authorship. Authors are distracted. Mistakes happen. Coincidences occur. Consideration of the accumulated weight of the evidence, however, makes it quite clear why the questions arose.

For non-Stratfordians the case for Will Shakspere as the poet/ dramatist fails because of the consistency and cumulative weight of the evidence against him. No single piece of evidence by itself is persuasive. What persuades is the way the evidence adds up, fact after fact, and the way the lack of evidence throws more and more doubt on the Stratfordian belief.

Conventional biographies ignore the cumulative weight, or cumulative absence, of the evidence. Individual pieces of negative evidence are treated separately. Each can then be discounted as coincidence, or unimportant, or uncorroborated, or a mistake, or unexceptional for the times, or admitting of other interpretations. Sometimes evidence is simply dismissed cavalierly with phrases such as "however that may be."

The biographies then move on to conjecture about what "must" have happened. This may be difficult to believe, but a reading of any of the standard biographies, whether as books or in introductions to the works, will show it to be generally true. The reader who is alert to distinguish facts from conjecture will see immediately that firm evidence of authorship for Will Shakspere of Stratford from his lifetime is nonexistent. The tip-off is the liberal use of "possibly," "undoubtedly," "perhaps," and the like on matters of great importance, such as Will Shakspere's education, his activity in the theater, and his position in London literary and court circles.

The dull facts of Will Shakspere's mundane biography add up to the life of a moneylender, real estate investor, grain dealer, theater personage, and possibly an actor, although of no fame whatsoever. Nothing in the historical records of his life has anything to do with anything literary. Nothing. Everything that should be found if he were the famous poet/playwright of London is missing. Only with the greatest difficulty can Will Shakspere—as described by the historical record of his lifetime in its entirety—be reconciled with the Elizabethan Renaissance genius who wrote *Hamlet, Lear, As You Like It, Romeo and Juliet, The Tempest,* as well as the incomparable *Sonnets.* Indeed, only by bestowing his name, modernized to Shakespeare, on the poems and plays can Will Shakspere be transformed into the author.

If that transformation is made, the reader then faces a daunting paradox. Will Shakspere of Stratford-on-Avon, when considered to be the author, successfully avoided putting his own life into his poems and plays. At the same time he wrote most knowledgeably and most extensively about the nobility, who led entirely different lives from his own. Perhaps it was a miracle of his genius, but genius needs something to work with. Will Shakspere's life story provides nothing of any significance for what is found in the poems and plays.

The nullity of his life has led to lopsided biographies. Pages after pages and whole chapters are devoted to his ancestors, parents, and relatives, life in Stratford, what the grammar school must have been like, conjecture about his twenties, the cryptic and allusive references to him, the construction of the theaters, the complex evolutions and fortunes of the acting companies, life in London under Elizabeth and James, the politics of the times, appreciations of the poems and plays, and on and on. All this peripheral scholarship overwhelms Will Shakspere, who seems to disappear from view. Reading a conventional biography of Will Shakspere as the man who is supposed to be the great poet/dramatist can be frustrating and profoundly unrewarding. The subject is missing from his own biography.

The mundane inconsequence of a life record devoid of anything literary has also led modern biographers to a strategic decision on orthography. They "modernize" or "normalize" Will Shakspere's name to "Shakespeare," thus automatically linking him to the poems and plays and obliterating any distinctions that might cause inconvenient questions. Much has been made about the wide variety of surname spellings in Elizabethan times; and it is certainly convenient (some would say self-serving) to modernize them all to one spelling. A simple analysis of the spellings and their usage does not, however, allow such a convenient conflation of the two names, which are similar, but different.

Chapter Three

Shakspere versus Shakespeare

Spelling was chaotic in Elizabethan times. There were no English dictionaries, no spelling books. Language was mostly oral and aural. For a large majority of the citizens, a word was primarily what it sounded like, not what it looked like. More than three-quarters of them could not read or write. Writers and printers decided how English would be spelled, and their opinions varied. Sometimes printers changed the spelling of a word so that it would fit on a line of type.

The spelling of proper names could be even more chaotic. Sir Walter Raleigh's name was also spelled Raliegh, Relegh, Raghley, Rawley, Rawly, Rawlie, Rawleigh, Raulighe, Raughlie, and Rayly. Members of the same immediate family spelled their surname in different ways. A man's name could be spelled in two different ways in the same document, even in the same sentence. Will Shakspere's name was no exception. Members of his extended family, if they could read, saw their surname spelled about a hundred different ways, ranging from Schackespeare to Shakspur.[1] By twentieth-century standards, all Elizabethans flunked spelling.

At first glance, the names Shakspere and Shakespeare might seem to be just two of the hundred or so spellings of the same family name. They then would be taken to designate the same man. This similarity in spellings has lent subtle and powerful support for the belief that Will Shakspere of Stratford wrote the works of Shakespeare. Closer analysis of the spellings and of which spellings were used when, however, reveals contrasting patterns of usage: The businessman was Shakspere; the writer was Shakespeare.

The name of the poet/dramatist, whoever he was, was spelled Shakespeare with great uniformity. That's how the name appeared on the title pages of the published works.[2] That's how the author's name appeared on his only dedications, those on his two narrative poems. That's how it was spelled on his *Sonnets*. That's how his contemporaries usually spelled it when they praised the author and his works in their poems and other writings.[3] In three dozen literary references to the author by name, the name is spelled Shakespeare about eighty-five percent of the time.[4]

About half the time the name Shake-speare was written with a hyphen. For Elizabethans a hyphenated name generally, if not always, meant that it was a made-up name or pseudonym. Hyphenation of Shake-speare's name was not an occasional lapse or an aberration or a typographical necessity; it occurred in almost half the instances, always by those who were printing the poems and plays or who were writing about them.[5] Will Shakspere's name was almost never hyphenated.

Given the chaotic spelling of the times, the uniform use of the name Shakespeare to designate the poet/dramatist is quite remarkable. The uniformity suggests that the name was not a family name subject to a variety of spellings by a variety of family members over the generations. The name appears to have been a made-up name used for a single purpose—to designate the author, whoever he was, of the poems and plays. For that purpose, printers spelled it the same way. They avoided the Shakspere spelling or one of its variants.

If the printers had *not* avoided the Shakspere spelling, if Will Shakespere's name in one of its variants had appeared on all the title pages of the poems and plays, or most of them, or even many of them, the usage would have specifically pointed to the man from Stratford as the author. That's the way his name was spelled there. But the name did not so appear. The name on Shakespeare's works was uniformly spelled Shakespeare.

To reverse the argument, if Will Shakspere of Stratford was indeed the author, then for some reason and somehow he was able to induce the London printers and most of the literary figures to spell his name Shakespeare on the poems and plays or when writing about them. That they would agree to this with such uniformity, avoiding the Stratford spelling with its many variants, strains belief.

If uniformity of spelling was the hallmark of the author's name, inconsistency plagued the Stratford man's name, a phenomenon not at all unusual in Elizabethan times. From his birth to his death, his name was spelled in at least fourteen different ways. Almost always, however, it was spelled Shakspere or one of the many variants, a spelling that reflected a pronunciation with a flat "a", as in "shack spur." In Elizabethan times, when most commoners were illiterate, pronunciation of a name came first, the spelling of it afterwards when it was required for legal documents. Only rarely was his name written Shakespeare, one of the many variations in spelling of the family name.

The Shakspere spelling was the most common spelling most closely associated with him as a person. His name was spelled Shakspere in the records of his baptism and his burial. Church, legal, and business records referred to the man from Stratford as Shakspere, Shakspear, Shexpere, and other variants, including occasionally Shakespeare and Shackespeare. In two-thirds of about sixty-five nonliterary records, his name is spelled Shakspere or one of its flat "a" variants.[6] Notably, the variant spellings of Shakspere for the man from Stratford continued even throughout the years when the poet/dramatist Shakespeare, as his name was uniformly spelled, was at the height of his success in London theater and literary circles.

Even in Will Shakspere's last years, the pattern was unchanged. After all Shakespeare's plays and poems had been written and half of them published to some acclaim, the man from Stratford, supposedly the author, persisted in using the name Shakspere or a variant. On his will the signatures were spelled—not Shakespeare—but Shakspere (twice) and Shakspeare. In the body of the will, written by an attorney, the spelling was Shack-speare, again a Stratfordian variant spelling.[7] The burial record reads: "Will. Shakspere gent." Even the inscription on the monument in Stratford, which has been widely understood to be some sort of tribute to the author Shakespeare, stuck with a variant of the Stratford spelling—Shakspeare.

Besides the signatures on the will, three other signatures, all from within four years of his death, are said to be authentic. These three are truncated to Shakspe (twice) and Shaksp, again Stratfordian variant spellings. He always accepted Shakspere or a variant as his name, even on his will, and so did those who kept records about him as the businessman and landowner from Stratford. The pattern is clear.[8]

In his works Shakespeare often accords high value to preserving one's good name and honor.[9] Everyone knows the passage from *Othello*: "Who steals my purse steals trash...but he that filches from me my good name robs me of that which not enriches him, and makes me poor indeed." If Will Shakspere was the author of that passage, he certainly was oddly indifferent to the use and spelling of his own name. In addition, the pattern would require belief that he reserved the Shakespeare spelling almost exclusively—and uniformly—for the poems and plays, but permitted the Stratford spelling for his business dealings. Then, despite the fame and fortune won by the Shakespeare by-line in London, he clung to the Stratford spelling even in his dying days. That he should treat his name in such a dichotomous way is hard to accept.

Equally difficult to accept is the proposition that the poet/dramatist who penned almost a million words of the most wonderful poetry never developed a distinctive, personal signature. The handwriting of many authors in all ages has often been difficult to read, sometimes almost illegible. Their signatures, however, almost always have a flow and style that are distinctive, even if they vary them on different kinds of documents. Will Shakspere's six purported signatures, however, do not bespeak a fluent writer. Even though they are fairly easy to read, they are spelled out awkwardly and indifferently.

The distinction between the two names is either ignored or

rejected in conventional Shakespearean biography. The biographers "modernize" or "normalize" the Stratford man's name to Shakespeare.[10] Normalizing to Shakespeare makes it easier on the reader, who is spared having to keep track of different spellings. It also allows biographers to avoid troublesome identity problems that are suggested by the different spellings. The normalized spelling is considered as just one of the variant spellings, conveniently overlooking the two different patterns of usage.

Modernizing the spelling shoves aside the distinction between the two names, a distinction that argues for two different people of widely different backgrounds. One name, Shakspere in various spellings, refers directly to an actual person; the other seems to be a pseudonym for a writer who cannot or does not wish to be acknowledged as such publicly.

Most biographies make no mention of the distinction and use the Shakespeare spelling throughout. Some do alert the reader. In her widely read biography, Marchette Chute simply states: "All spelling has been modernized. This service is habitually done for Shakespeare, and there seems to be no reason to fail to do it for his contemporaries."

The problem is described in revealing terms by Professor Gary Taylor, a leading Stratfordian scholar in the late twentieth century:

The spelling of Shakespeare's name causes special difficulties. I had originally intended to spell the name as erratically in my own prose as in the historical record, changing the spelling whenever one of my quoted sources did so; this has the desirable effect of continually deconstructing a reader's confidence in the familiar "Shakespeare." However, it soon becomes—as my publisher pointed out—an irritating distraction. "Shakspere," which seems to have been his own preferred spelling, would be disconcerting for a modern reader, without the advantage of reflecting past practice. In the end I have had to concede that my work, like all those it discusses, is the product of its own time. In our time "Shakespeare" is normal, and I have therefore grudgingly perpetuated it.

The reader, however, doesn't learn about Taylor's reluctant decision until the very last paragraph of his 414-page book, *Reinventing Shakespeare*, a cultural history of Shakespeare studies and stage performances down through the centuries.

Distinguishing between the two names is essential for any rational discussion of the authorship issue. The point at issue is whether two different people are involved. To use the modernized spelling of Shakespeare for both the Stratford man and the author, whoever he was, would hopelessly confuse any discussion. Stalwart Stratfordians sometimes object to the use of locutions such as the Stratford man or the glove maker's son or even the spelling Shakspere as terms that unfairly discriminate against their view that Will Shakspere of Stratford was Shakespeare the poet/dramatist. They argue that it tends to prejudice the discussion.

Distinguishing between the spellings, however, makes sense for several reasons. As noted, it is essential for any rational discussion, and the Shakspere spelling was, in fact, the most common spelling of the name of the man from Stratford. Making the distinction also gains legitimacy from traditional Shakespearean studies. In the late nineteenth century, establishment scholars who believed firmly in the Stratford man as the author often used the Stratfordian spelling for the poet/dramatist's name, usually spelling it Shakspere or Shaksper. These writers and scholars included the poets Keats and Coleridge, the historian Carlyle, Shakspereans Knight and Dowden, and the New Shakspere Society. The society's position was proclaimed by F. J. Furnivall in his founder's note:

> This spelling of our great Poet's name is taken from the only unquestionably genuine signatures of his that we possess, the three on his will and the two on his Stratford conveyance and mortgage....Though it has hitherto been too much to ask people to suppose that SHAKSPERE knew how to spell his own name, I hope the demand may not prove too great for the Membership of the New Society.[11]

Only in the twentieth century, coincidental with the strong candidacy of the earl of Oxford as the true author, have most of the establishment scholars balked at using the Shakspere spelling for the author whose byline was spelled Shakespeare.

Will Shakspere's mundane life, its missing literary content, and the distinctly different usage of the names Shakspere and Shakespeare have called in question Will Shakspere's credentials as the great poet/dramatist. The questioning is not new. It started in earnest in the mid-nineteenth century. Despite decades of energetic efforts, however, the doubters and dissenters have not been able to topple Will Shakspere of Stratford-on-Avon from his pedestal as the immortal Bard.

Chapter Four

The Case for Will Shakspere as Author

For nearly four hundred years, Will Shakspere of Stratford-on-Avon, the man of mundane inconsequence in the documentary record, has remained on his pedestal as the author of the works of Shakespeare. There must be a reason.

Similarity of name has been crucial. Its importance should not be underestimated. In conventional scholarship, the name Shakespeare is simply one of many spellings that were common for the times. After all, Christopher Marlowe's name was spelled more than a dozen different ways; two spellings appear in a single sentence in a legal document. Edward de Vere, seventeenth earl of Oxford, spelled his title at least five different ways, including Oxinforde.

So, the scholars conclude, Shakespeare/Shakspere, no matter what the spelling, wrote the poems and plays. The distinctive pattern in the different spellings—one usage for the man from Stratford and the other for the author—is not considered significant, when considered at all. The general reader, interested primarily in the poems and plays, seldom has any reason to question the assumption that the man from Stratford-on-Avon whose name was usually spelled Shakspere was the same man as the poet/dramatist known uniformly as Shakespeare.

Sheer momentum has certainly been a major factor. English professors and literary critics have published tens of thousands of scholarly books and articles—all written on the assumption that the Stratford man was the author. Publishers have taken academia at its word. Every single one of the collected works of Shakespeare, every edition of the individual plays, every edition of the poems, all of them assume that Will Shakspere of Stratford-on-Avon was the author. A short version of the same Stratfordian story is often tucked into the program notes for Shakespeare stage performances.

Secondary schools, colleges, and universities, almost without exception, teach that Shakespeare was the man from Stratford. It's an appealing story, with democratic overtones, of a commoner from a rural town who makes a small fortune and wins eternal fame in the theater. From all this it follows that there must be some historical, documentary foundation, however shaky, for the general belief that the works of Shakespeare were written by Will Shakspere of Stratford.

For the general reader the most persuasive argument is probably the simple, straightforward fact that at his death and for almost two centuries afterwards, no one publicly questioned whether Will Shakspere was the author of the poems and plays of Shakespeare. If any of his contemporaries wanted to express doubts, the time to do it was at his death or after publication of his collected plays in the *First Folio*. No one did. No other writer went on the record to claim that he himself was the author, nor did his friends, relatives, or descendants. (Nor, it must be said, did Will Shakspere ever claim to be the author.) As Will Shakspere's survivors and contemporaries died out, no one raised any questions about the identity of the author, or if they did no word of it remains. The few writers, antiquarians, and theater people in the next generations who left any record of their opinions expressed no reservations. Evidently, for anyone who cared, there was no reason to question the identity of the author of the works of Shakespeare.

As the decades passed, it was generally accepted that Will Shakspere wrote the works of Shakespeare. As the centuries passed, the general acceptance became a firmly entrenched belief, part of the culture of Western civilization. By the end of the eighteenth century, the belief had soared into Bardolatry. His ardent worshippers deified Shakespeare as the Divine, the Immortal Bard of Avon. Stratford-on-Avon became their shrine.

At the start, this unquestioning acceptance was aided by historical events. For nearly twenty years (1642–1660) the public theaters were closed under Puritan rule. Stage plays and entertainment were anathema. Memories faded. No one paid much attention, if any, to Shakespeare's life story or identity. There was no literary biography, only anecdotes and random observations, some possibly true, most not. Even most Stratfordian scholars do not put great store in them as evidence. For the rest of the century only three men left brief biographical notes; none is considered reliable. Two of them were not published until more than a century later.[1]

Not until 1709—almost a century after Will Shakspere's death—was anything significant published about his life. Nicholas Rowe wrote a short biographical sketch, which included some mistakes and unverified legends, for his edition of the collected plays. Despite its brevity and inaccuracy, his account remained the standard for a hundred years. No one did any biographical research, with one exception. A clergyman launched an investigation in and around Stratford, but he concluded that Will Shakspere was *not* the author. He suppressed his conclusion, which remained hidden for more than a century.[2]

At about the same time, Shakespeare's plays began to be more popular, largely through the efforts of David Garrick, a consummate self-promoter and the most famous actor/director of the century. Garrick also put Stratford-on-Avon on the tourist map by staging the first Shakespeare festival in 1769, thus launching what has been called "the Shakespeare industry." Even before the start of the nineteenth century Shakespeare had been deified, and Bardolatry founded.

Not until 1821—more than two centuries after Will Shakspere's death—was there a thoroughly researched, scholarly biography. The author, Edmund Malone, a prodigious Shakespearean editor, died before finishing his work, which ultimately filled a seven-hundred-page volume. The several hundred pages he did finish took Will Shakspere only to the beginning of "the Lost

Years" of his twenties. James Boswell the younger completed it. By the mid-nineteenth century, biography had begun to take on the scope and authority that are characteristic of modern scholarship. Scholars began to focus on primary sources and analyze the documentary record.

So intense was the research for historical information that at least two Stratfordian scholars became forgers. For a time, their forgeries were widely accepted as new evidence adding to what was known about Will Shakspere and generally confirming the views of conventional Shakespearean scholarship. Their fraudulent "discoveries" made them famous in antiquarian and literary circles; they were heroes. Eventually, they were exposed, but their clever forgeries of dozens of documents purportedly about Shakespeare's life and work clouded scholarship well into the twentieth century. Some Oxfordians believe that Shakespearean scholarship continues to be tainted by the forgeries.[3]

At the same time, universities were introducing courses in English literature. Until then, there had been no study of English literature as such, no literary criticism in classrooms, no literary biography. But now academics in universities began erecting the scholarly apparatus of primary source research, graduate studies, journal articles, and doctorate degrees. In English literature courses, the Bard of Avon was the reigning monarch, and Shakespearean scholarship was built on the long-held belief, an almost religious conviction, that Will Shakspere was the author.

The scholars who inherited the unquestioned belief in the Divine Bard of Avon found documentary support for their faith primarily in three places: *Greenes Groatsworth of Wit*, with its allusion to "Shake-scene"; the burial monument in Stratford-on-Avon; and the testimony in the *First Folio.*[4]

THE "SHAKE-SCENE" ALLUSION

Shakespeare biographers lay great importance on an allusion to an unidentified actor described as an "upstart crow" and a "Shake-scene" in *Greenes Groatsworth of Wit*, published in 1592 by Henry Chettle. For them, it marks Will Shakspere's first appearance in London after seven years of total obscurity. He turned twenty-eight that year.

The cryptic Shake-scene allusion is interpreted as proving that an actor with a name like that was on the London stage and that he also was a bold and budding playwright. The interpretation is crucial for the Stratfordian case because it alone can be read to make the linkage of actor to author during Will Shakspere's lifetime. If the author of the poems and plays is the actor—and Will Shakspere may have been a bit-part actor—then the case for him as author becomes more credible. Biographer Sidney Lee writes: "It is obvious that Shakespeare [i.e. Will Shakspere] at the time of Chettle's apology was winning a high reputation alike as actor, man and writer." Bentley says the passage "made clear the identity of the actor-turned-playwright." Levin says it "is clearly a protest against a mere actor who has presumed to become a playwright."[5] The crucial interpretation is "obvious" and "clear" for most academic Stratfordians. Professor Schoenbaum does recognize "many ambiguities and perplexities," but he, too, reads the passage as support for Will Shakspere as both actor and playwright.

Groatsworth was published by Henry Chettle, a playwright and printer, in the year Will Shakspere turned twenty-eight.[6] Some scholars suspect that Chettle wrote the booklet, too, foisting it on the public as the deathbed work of the impoverished playwright, Robert Greene.[7] The Shake-scene allusion in it is actually an attack on actors who have the effrontery to imitate playwrights. Chettle's own letter of apology for the attack followed a few months later. In it he even acknowledged that some readers thought that he himself was the author of *Groatsworth*.

In typically convoluted Elizabethan prose, the Shake-scene passage warns three unnamed playwrights not to trust actors, particularly "an upstart crow, beautified with our feathers that with his tiger's heart wrapped in a player's hide" fancies himself "well able to bombast out a blank verse as the best of you, and...the only Shake-scene in a country." The "tiger's heart" allusion is a parody of a line in Shakespeare's *Henry VI Part 3*. Chettle's apology for this attack on Shake-scene the upstart actor was addressed to one of the playwrights, still unnamed. These are the passages cited by Stratfordian scholars to construct the equation that Will Shakspere = actor = Shake-scene = dramatist = Shakespeare. (Readers who want to test the validity and strength of the equation for themselves will find the texts in appendix B.)

For Stratfordian scholars, it is crucial that the passages be interpreted in a way that proves the equation to be true. And, in fact, they insist that the passages are "obvious" and "clear." If their interpretation is not true, then Will Shakspere's life is devoid of anything literary. No other evidence from his lifetime links him personally as an actual person living and working in London to the writing of Shakespeare's poems and plays. The names are similar, but that's all.

The interpretation of the passages, however, may well be mistaken. The misreading was first flagged in the late nineteenth century. Even though a few Stratfordians have acknowledged the misreading, the vast majority in academia have continued to adhere to the conventional interpretation.[8]

Non-Stratfordians, however, reject that interpretation as proving anything about authorship. Through careful analysis of the convoluted texts, Ogburn demonstrates how they have been misread, confusing the unnamed actor, Shake-scene, with one of the three unnamed playwrights and inferring that both were Will Shakspere. Take away the misreadings, Ogburn says, "and nothing during Shakspere's life remains to suggest even remotely that he was a writer—and little enough that he was an actor." Whatever can be made of the disputed passages, they hardly provide clear and obvious evidence of authorship. The writing is deliberately cryptic. No names are named. Nothing says Shake-scene came from Stratford. Far from being a fairly clear identification, it is deliberately evasive and obscure.

MONUMENTAL EVIDENCE

Between the cryptic Shake-scene allusion in 1592 and publication of the *First Folio* thirty-one years later, only one other record is cited regularly as evidence that Will Shakspere of Stratford-on-Avon was the poet/dramatist: his monument in the church there.[9] For at least two centuries the bust in the monument has depicted a high-browed man with pen and paper, clearly a writer. Shakespeare was a writer. Underneath the bust, the epitaph is addressed to Will Shakspere by name, and in one of the Stratford variant spellings, Shakspeare (although his first name is omitted). Will Shakspere was baptized, married, and buried in Stratford-on-Avon, therefore he must be the famous author depicted in the monument.

Two lines in Latin in the monument's inscription compare him to Nestor for judgment, to Socrates for genius, and to Virgil for poetic art, and they place him on Mount Olympus. Professor Bevington, one of the few to comment on it, says that these two Latin lines "indicate the high reputation he enjoyed at the time of his death." The six-line epitaph in English ends by saying that all he wrote "leaves living art, but page, to serve his wit." For Stratfordians, the Latin and English lines obviously refer to the art, writings, and genius of the Stratford man who is buried nearby.

Stratfordian scholars, however, have almost totally ignored the substance of the inscription. Although they do offer opinions, some reverent, some scathing, on the effigy as it appears in the twentieth century, they are notably reticent about the meaning of the inscription. Even Bevington, who has something to say about the Latin, says nothing about the six lines in English. Most biographers offer nothing at all about it; many don't even provide the text, even though it runs only eight lines.[10]

For Oxfordians, of course, the monument and its inscription are more significant for the questions they raise than as evidence for Will Shakspere as author. As discussed in chapter 2, the Latin comparisons are not made to the appropriate ancients. The English verse is cryptic, confused, and contradictory. It never mentions plays, poems, or the theater. The inscription seems woefully inadequate for a famous author. Most significant of all, the effigy with pen and paper is almost certainly not the original, which depicted a dour man without pen or paper.

Besides the external evidence of *Groatsworth* and the monument in Stratford-on-Avon, devoted Stratfordian scholars find internal evidence in the poems and plays. They cite allusions in Shakespeare that seem to reflect the life of Will Shakspere of Stratford-on-Avon. They have collected references to leather-working, his father's trade, and to schoolboys, assuming he went to school. They cite allusions to hunting and gardening, rural pastimes appropriate for the Stratford man. One reads a Shakespearean image of an eddy under a bridge as reflecting an eddy under the bridge in Stratford-on-Avon. A girl named Katherine Hamlet reportedly drowned in the River Avon when Will Shakspere was thirteen; in Shakespeare's *Hamlet*, young Ophelia drowns herself. Most Shakespearean scholars, however, do not make much of the allusions. Some dismiss them as amounting to very little.[11]

Analysis of the Stratfordian case for Will Shakspere as the author does not inspire much confidence. The similarity of names—Shakspere and Shakespeare—seems to reinforce the case but, in fact, is deceptive; the names were different. The historical evidence offered to support Will Shakspere's position on his pedestal crumbles under examination. The differences between the Stratford man and the poet/dramatist loom larger.

During Will Shakspere's lifetime, nothing connects him securely to the famous poet/dramatist of London. *Groatsworth* is cryptic in the extreme; the Stratford monument's effigy is suspect and its inscription unhelpfully banal. Between the publication of *Groatsworth*, when Will Shakspere was twenty-eight, and his death at fifty-two, no records at all can be cited to link him unambiguously to the works of Shakespeare. There are many literary references and allusions to Shakespeare the author, but not one of them connects him historically to the man from Stratford. For those last twenty-four years of Will Shakspere's life, what the fairly extensive records do depict is a life completely at variance with that of a famous author of genius. It is the life of a moneylender, real estate investor, grain dealer, and theater personage.

During his career, Shakespeare, whoever he was, achieved a certain amount of fame as the accomplished author of London. His plays were performed regularly; some were printed in multiple editions. The narrative poems with his dedications were reprinted many times. His contemporaries noted the excellence of his poems and his plays. Never, however, did they leave word that the poet/dramatist Shakespeare was from Stratford-on-

Avon or mention anything about him that might identify the author as the man from Stratford.

Given this dearth of evidence, the testimony in the prefatory material to the *First Folio*, published seven years after he died, becomes crucial for those who argue that the evidence supports Will Shakspere as the author of the works of Shakespeare.

Chapter Five

The Ambiguous Testimony of the *First Folio*

On and off, starting in 1621 and extending into 1623, four printers in London were hard at work on a major publishing project: *Mr. William Shakespeares Comedies, Histories & Tragedies, Published According to the True Original Copies.* Collected in the book were thirty-six plays by Shakespeare; half of them were seeing print for the first time.

Much later, scholars nicknamed the book the *First Folio* from the way it was laid out and printed. Four large pages printed on both sides of a single sheet of paper folded once is called a folio. Two columns of type filled each folio page, which was about thirteen inches high by eight inches wide. In the decade that followed publication of the *First Folio*, the collected plays were printed again in editions now called the second, third, and fourth folios.

The printers, who had other projects as well, took more than a year to produce the thick volume of 908 pages. The type was hand-set by as many as nine different compositors, each with his own ideas about spelling and punctuation. They changed words to make lines fit. Proofreading was haphazard. Errors and variations in spelling and punctuation abound in all the extant copies.[1]

Printers had made great strides in the century and a half since Gutenberg, but by twentieth-century standards printing was still primitive. Every copy undoubtedly was somewhat different from every other copy because the printers stopped the presses continually throughout the process to make changes and corrections. One play, *Troilus and Cressida*, never did appear in the index; it was added to the volume after the index page had been printed.

Estimates of the print-runs range from 750 to 1,200 copies. Less than 240 survived the centuries. The Folger Shakespeare Library in Washington, D.C., has acquired eighty-two copies in various conditions, thirteen of them complete.

The first dozen pages of the *First Folio* provide the most powerful testimony supporting the widely accepted belief that Will Shakspere wrote Shakespeare.[2] Therein are found the famous (or infamous) portrait, five commendatory poems, two open letters, an index, and a list of actors who performed in the plays.

Ben Jonson, the de facto poet laureate, provided a short poem opposite the portrait and a longer one in memory of the author, whom he must have known, although there is no direct evidence for it.[3] Leonard Digges, whose stepfather was an overseer of Will Shakspere's will, also contributed a memorial poem.[4] John Heminge and Henry Condell, the two players mentioned belatedly in Will Shakspeare's will, signed one dedicatory letter to the book's patrons and another that was addressed to the general reader. The testimony of these four men is crucial to the case for Will Shakspere as the author.

The title page of the *First Folio* displays an engraved portrait of the author. It depicts a well-to-do commoner, perfectly appropriate for Will Shakspere. As far as the records show, the portrait did not draw objections from the many who must have known the author, whoever he was. Both the portrait and the half-length bust in the Stratford monument appeared within seven years of Will Shakspere's death. If someone else was the author, no contemporary or anyone who might have known or seen the author left any word that the portrait, or the bust, did not depict the true author.

In the *First Folio*, and for the first time, close connections were made between the plays of Shakespeare and Will Shakspere. Ben

Jonson in his poem of praise calls the author the "sweet swan of Avon." Leonard Digges writes that through his works Shakespeare's name will outlive his tomb even when "time dissolves thy Stratford moniment." When Jonson's reference to "Avon" is joined to Digges's "Stratford," Shakespeare's hometown is identified. Jonson's line, "And though thou hadst small Latin and less Greek," seems to jibe with Will Shakspere's lack of a university education.

One page in the *First Folio* lists "the principal actors in all these plays"; William Shakespeare leads the list of twenty-six actors, and with a specially designed "W" for his first name. Among the actors listed are John Heminge, Henry Condell, and Richard Burbage, the same three who were in the late addition to Will Shakspere's will. A dedicatory letter over the names of Heminge and Condell states that they collected the plays "only to keep the memory of so worthy a friend and fellow alive as was our Shakespeare." These multiple references all point to the theater personage from Stratford-on-Avon as the author.

For the first time, everything seems to come together here for Will Shakspere: allusions to the River Avon and to his Stratford monument, references to him as a fellow actor, and a portrait that was apparently accepted as authentic. The publication of the thirty-six plays of Shakespeare in the *First Folio* provided the opportunity for the true author, if he was someone else and still alive, or for his friends and family, to denounce as false the attribution to the man from Stratford. As far as the record shows, no one stepped forward to contradict Ben Jonson openly. No one questioned the testimony of the *First Folio*. No one corrected the record.

Non-Stratfordians disagree. They note that the *First Folio*, which provides no biographical information, poses a number of problems that undercut its authority. They maintain that in every instance the testimony that purports to identify Will Shakspere as the author is ambiguous or not to be trusted.

Ben Jonson's major role in the publication of the *First Folio* raises the first of the problems. Eight years younger than Will Shakspere, he was the leading literary figure of his time, a celebrity who became the unofficial poet laureate. Never during Will Shakspere's lifetime, however, did Ben Jonson publish anything mentioning Shakespeare—not even at Will Shakspere's death, the year Jonson became poet laureate. (No one else did, either.) In that same year he published poems addressed to Greene, Beaumont, and Peele, but none to Shakespaere. To be sure, Ben Jonson and Shakespeare are thought to have been rivals, but Jonson was never shy about criticizing or commenting on other writers. He was the greatest literary critic of the age. On Shakespeare during his lifetime, however, Jonson was silent. Only seven years after Will Shakspere's death did Jonson find reason to praise him, and then he did so with extravagant praise that was totally inconsistent with his prior silence.

Although Jonson published nothing about Shakespeare by name until the *First Folio,* he did make two allusions earlier that can be read as comments on Will Shakspere of Stratford-on-Avon. Both, however, are satirical and derogatory. One mocks his pretentions to a coat of arms that seemed to have the motto "Not Without Right." A character in one of Jonson's plays says it should be "Not Without Mustard." The other is a poem called "On Poet-Ape" that ridicules an unnamed playwright who apes poet/dramatists by stealing old plays. Scholarly opinion is split on whether Jonson was referring to Shakspere/Shakespeare or to someone else.[5]

The hard fact remains that Ben Jonson's only two recorded comments on Shakespeare by name, besides those in the posthumous *First Folio* preface, also came after Will Shakspere's death; and neither comment was published by Jonson. The first was in a conversation noted by a Scots poet. The comment was brief but critical: Jonson told the Scotsman that Shakespeare "wanted [lacked] art," and that he put a shipwreck in Bohemia a hundred miles from the sea.[6] That's all.

The other was a long, rambling, highly cryptic notebook entry by Jonson that was written years after Will Shakspere's death and probably after the *First Folio* was published. It seems to be a half-hearted, self-justifying apology for his treatment of Shakespeare; it almost defies explication. Included in it is the famous line "(for I loved the man, and do honour his memory (on this side idolatry) as much as any)." Delivering his praise parenthetically and then hedging it in parentheses within parentheses may or may not be significant, but Jonson, like most writers of the day, was a master at convoluted equivocation. The rest of the passage is convoluted in the extreme and generally seems rather pejorative. Such was the literary figure chosen to write the major prefatory poems for the collected plays of Shakespeare. (See appendix C for the text of *Timber*.)

The portrait in the *First Folio* is accompanied by a ten-line poem "To the Reader" supplied by Ben Jonson. Paradoxically, it rejects the portrait. Placed opposite the portrait, it steers the reader away from it. The poem opens by stating that the portrait was "for gentle Shakespeare cut," a portrait *for* him, not *of* him. After noting the difficulty the engraver had in making the figure "out-do the life," and wishing that the engraver had drawn Shakespeare's "wit" as well as his face, Jonson concludes: "But, since he cannot, reader, look not on his picture but his book."[7]

Jonson's going to such trouble to advise the reader to reject the portrait is strange, unless he wanted to drop a hint that the engraving was not a likeness of the man who wrote the plays. The engraver, moreover, was just fifteen years old when Will Shakspere died. There's no reason to believe he ever met his subject and every reason to ask why the publishers did not commission a better artist.

The portrait engraving itself has puzzled those who examine it closely.[8] The right side of the front of Shakespeare's tunic is represented by what would be the left side of the back of the tunic. The face seems to have two right eyes. A curving line from the left ear to the chin gives the face itself the appearance of a mask. The whole head and ruff collar seem to be disengaged from the body and floating above the shoulders. Oxfordians, of course, call attention to the masklike face that might be hiding the face of the true author.[9]

Ben Jonson's longer, memorial poem of forty couplets is the most quoted tribute to the poet/dramatist. In it, Shakespeare is "the soul of the age! the applause! the delight! the wonder of our stage!" Jonson would have the ancient classical playwrights return "to hear thy buskin tread, and shake a stage." The lavish praise, however, is in stark contrast to Jonson's silence about Shakespeare's poems and plays throughout the lifetime of the

The engraving on the title page of Shakespeare's *First Folio*, by Marcus Droesh-out, who was only fifteen when Will Shakspere died. In his poem on the facing page Ben Jonson advises readers to "look not on his picture, but his book." Among the curious anomalies: the right front of his doublet depicts what would be the left rear of a doublet. His head seems disengaged from his body. His face appears almost to be a mask. The portrait is notably plain and unembellished, totally lacking the elaborate adornments created for other title pages of the time. (By permission of the Folger Shakespeare Library.)

poet/dramatist. His only other comments were the one or two literary allusions disparaging the man from Stratford and the two unpublished comments after Will Shakspere died.

In his memorial poem Ben Jonson makes several allusions that Stratfordians read as linking the plays of Shakespeare to the man from Stratford. The allusions, however, are not without ambiguity. The one cited most often is probably the line, "And though thou hadst small Latin and less Greek," which leads into praise of Shakespeare's creative genius. Stratfordian scholars take it as referring to Will Shakspere's lack of a higher education. The grammar, however, allows at least two other interpretations. One maintains that the word "though" means "even if," so the clause should be read "even if you had small Latin and less Greek, which is not the case." Thus Jonson could also have been saying that Shakespeare, whoever he was, did indeed have a higher education with advanced work in Latin and Greek. Another interpretation of the passage maintains that "small Latin and less Greek" refers, not to the playwright at all, but to Marlowe, Kyd, and Lyly in the previous lines. So it's not clear that Ben Jonson was referring unambiguously to Will Shakspere's lack of higher education; he could have had a highly educated author in mind, too. The seventeenth earl of Oxford, for example.[10]

The short epistle "To the Great Variety of Readers" signed by Heminge and Condell makes three major points, but all three are at variance with the facts. First, it exhorts readers several times to buy the book: "But, whatever you do, buy." The book, however, would have been quite expensive for the average reader to buy if priced to recover costs. And if a patron had covered most of the costs, which is more likely, there would have been no need to urge everybody three times to buy it. The insistent commercialism has a false ring to it.

Next, the letter expresses the wish that the author had lived to set forth and oversee publication of his plays. But Will Shakspere lived in prosperous semiretirement in Stratford-on-Avon for years after the last plays were written. There is no apparent reason he could not have prepared the plays for publication, if he wanted to. And if they were his.

Then comes a claim that is flatly contradicted by the facts. The letter says the two players took "maimed and deformed" versions of the plays and now offer them "cured, and perfect" in the *First Folio,* just as the author would have wanted them to be. The same claim is made in a headline on the title page, directly above the portrait. It says the plays were "published according to the true original copies." All scholars take these to be false and exaggerated promotional claims, since many of the texts are based on corrupt versions and are full of errors and misprints. For some plays the earlier quarto editions provide texts that are considered superior.

If Heminge and Condell wrote the letter and were the editors of the *First Folio,* as they claim, they were not honest about their undertaking. Nor is there any indication that they had any experience or talent for preparing such a massive work for publication. Heminge later became a grocer, and Condell ran a pub.

After such false testimony and self-serving claims, it's doubtful that the two letters signed by the actors should be trusted when they claim the plays were by "so worthy a friend and fellow...as was our Shakespeare," their "Shakespeare" supposedly being the man from Stratford who remembered them belatedly in his will.

The most significant deception, moreover, is that the two letters signed by Heminge and Condell were almost certainly written by Ben Jonson. Textual analysis of the letters has revealed Jonson's ghostwriting hand. Stratfordian scholars themselves discovered and have accepted this deception, even though it tends to raise questions about what Ben Jonson was up to in the *First Folio* and about his major, but problematic, role in the publishing venture.[11] Non-Stratfordian critics make the additional observation that Heminge and Condell were the same two actors whose names were added belatedly between the lines to Will Shakspere's will. Their names, along with Burbage's, constitute the only linkage in the will between Will Shakspere and the theater.

The most direct links in the *First Folio* between Shakespeare's plays and Will Shakspere of Stratford-on-Avon are the allusions to the River Avon and to Stratford. Or so it would seem. The allusions, however, come separately in two different poems, and again are ambiguous. In his poem, Jonson calls Shakespeare the "sweet swan of Avon." Three pages later, Leonard Digges, in his poem, says Shakespeare's name will endure when "time dissolves thy Stratford moniment." Only if the separate mentions are brought together and spliced with hyphens plus the addition of the preposition "on" can they be read as the name of Will Shakspere's hometown. Nowhere in the *First Folio* is the author directly identified as a native of Stratford-on-Avon, nor are his birth and death dates given, nor is any biographical information provided.

Oxfordians reject the notion that the lexical splice renders the only reading of the two lines by the two poets. They submit that the two allusions, read separately, could also have been pointing to a different man. Edward de Vere, seventeenth earl of Oxford, inherited and owned for some time a large estate on the banks of the River Avon about twenty miles upstream from Will Shakspere's obscure home town.[12] Conceivably, he, too, could be the "sweet swan of Avon." And a different Stratford, a well-known London suburb, was the town nearest the house where Oxford spent the last decade of his life while presumably revising and completing the plays. Readers of the *First Folio* might be more likely to think of that suburban Stratford, a few hours from the center of London, than the obscure town of Stratford-on-Avon, a four-day journey away.

Both Leonard Digges and Ben Jonson referred in their poems to the author's "moniment," as they wrote it before scholars modernized the spelling to monument. Digges called it "thy Stratford moniment"; Jonson wrote, "Thou art a moniment without a tomb." Jonson's line immediately raises a question because Will Shakspere, of course, is supposed to have had a tomb. It's under the unnamed slab in Trinity church at Stratford, just a few yards from his monument on the wall. The question is why Jonson would say Shakespeare is a "moniment without a tomb."

It's possible that both writers used the word moniment with deliberate ambiguity. They may not have been referring solely and necessarily to the monument in Stratford-on-Avon. The word moniment was a word with several dictionary meanings. Some, but not all, were similar to those of monument.

Ruth Loyd Miller, a leading Oxfordian scholar, notes that as Latinists Jonson and Digges would have known the difference between the two words. Moniment, not an unusual word in Elizabethan times, could mean a memorial or it could mean something narrated, such as a story. Both poets might have claimed, if challenged, that they were using the word moniment in its second sense and were referring to Shakespeare's written works, not to a stone monument in Trinity Church at Stratford-on-Avon.[13]

So, when Ben Jonson writes, "Thou art a moniment without a tomb," he could have meant that the author's essence was in his written works, his "moniment," and that he had no tomb. As it happens, the location of the final resting place of the seventeeth earl of Oxford is uncertain.

And, when Digges writes "thy Stratford moniment," he could have been addressing the seventeenth earl of Oxford, who lived his last decade at Hackney, just a mile or two from the well-known London suburb of Stratford. His "Stratford moniment" then would be the plays and poems he could have been finishing and revising before his death there. In this alternative reading, Digges would be saying that through the published plays Oxford's name must outlive his tomb "when that stone is rent and time dissolves thy Stratford moniment"—his moniment written in the London suburb of Stratford. Or Digges could have been referring to Will Shakspere's stone monument in Stratford-on-Avon. Readers could take their choice.[14]

It's possible, of course, that it's just coincidence that Oxford had an estate on the River Avon and a house near suburban Stratford. It's possible, too, that Jonson and Digges were thinking of the stone monument when they used the word moniment. And Digges does mention a tombstone being split and time dissolving the moniment. No direct evidence has been found to tell what they had in mind when they wrote, or how readers of the time might have interpreted their words. Still, the possible double meanings are provocative.

If any of the testimony in the *First Folio* were clear and unequivocal, the case for Will Shakspere as the poet/dramatist would be much more powerful. But it's not. The testimony is badly tainted by falsehoods, ambiguity, and potential double meanings. Ben Jonson's vague and ambiguous testimony about Shakespeare's identity is particularly suspect, given the total silence in all the years preceding his belated outburst of praise. Tellingly, he advises the reader to reject the portrait in the *First Folio* as that of the author. The self-proclaimed editors, Heminge and Condell, show themselves to be untrustworthy, thus throwing doubt on their claim that their friend was the author. They didn't even write the letters to which their names were attached. References to Shakespeare as the sweet swan of Avon with a Stratford moniment can point either to Will Shakspere or, possibly, to the seventeenth earl of Oxford. It is very difficult to accept the testimony at face value. It is almost as difficult to escape the suspicion that Will Shakspere may have been subtly set up as the decoy author, the front man for the true author who, for some reason, was to remain officially hidden.

For Stratfordians the *First Folio* and the Stratford monument provide the most obvious and most powerful direct testimony that Will Shakspere of Stratford was the famous dramatist. For non-Stratfordians the same *First Folio* testimony, combined with the mundane inconsequence of Will Shakspere's life records, casts serious doubt on his authorship. For the general reader, the challenge is to weigh the evidence presented by the scholars on both sides of the issue.

Assessing the cumulative weight of the evidence is crucial. Any single argument by itself can be denied or dismissed on some basis. For example, there is nothing literary in the life records of Will Shakspere of Stratford-on-Avon, but that in and of itself may not be enough to cast doubt upon his authorship. Maybe all traces of just those records that would have proved his literary achievements have been lost. Everything that might be expected if he were the author is missing, but just those records, too, might have been lost. The tremendous silence at his death might have resulted from his dying so far from London in a small town where nobody appreciated his achievements. The difference between the uniform spelling of Shakespeare on the author's works and the different spellings of Shakspere on the records of the man from Stratford might be an aberration or maybe even a peculiar preference by Will Shakspere, which everyone honored. The mediocre inscription on the Stratford monument might have been the result of ignorance. The early engravings of it showing a man with a wool or grain sack might have been mistaken. The engraver of the *First Folio* portrait might have been a poor choice, who botched the job. The ambiguous passages in the *First Folio* might have been nothing more than inscrutable but innocent Elizabethan wordplay. Maybe Shakespeare did deserve pride of place among the twenty-six actors listed in the *First Folio* who performed in his plays, even though no record lists him in any role in any play.

Any *single* argument aganst Will Shakspere's authorship can be countered by explanations that have some plausibility. The explanations, however, do little more than dismiss or deny each of the arguments as irrelevant or an aberration or insignificant or mistaken. For many who look into the authorship question the cumulative weight of the evidence against Will Shakspere is most persuasive.

For Oxfordians, the *First Folio* contains strong evidence that another Elizabethan, namely Edward de Vere, seventeenth earl of Oxford, was the true author. For them the most striking fact about the *First Folio* is that the two men to whom it was dedicated, and who probably financed it, were none other than a son-in-law of Oxford and the son-in-law's brother. Thus, heirs of Oxford were closely involved in the publication of Shakespeare's plays.

Part Two

THE LEADING CHALLENGER: THE EARL OF OXFORD

Chapter Six

The Search for the True Author

One day in April 1786 two American diplomats stopped for the night in Stratford-on-Avon. They were not there on business as emissaries for their infant nation but as tourists, to visit the famous Birthplace of the Bard of Avon. Stratford was already becoming famous as a tourist town. Seventeen years earlier, the "Shakespeare Industry" had been launched in earnest with the Shakespeare Jubilee celebration staged there by the actor and theater promoter David Garrick.

The two diplomats were John Adams and Thomas Jefferson, who would become the second and third presidents of the United States. Jefferson's only record of the visit is what today would be called his expense account. John Adams made some notes in his diary, but he was not impressed by what he saw:

> There is nothing preserved of this great genius which is worth knowing—nothing which might inform us what education, what company, what accident turned his mind to letters and the drama. His name is not even on his gravestone. An ill sculptured head is set up by his wife by the side of his grave in the church.

Adams then concludes by noting that the sculpture cannot do justice to Shakespeare's fame; his genius is "immortal."[1]

Adams was not alone in his misgivings about what he could discover about "this great genius." The same year saw publication of a historical allegory called *The Story of the Learned Pig*. In it, the anonymous author makes a mock confession that he himself wrote five plays of "the immortal Shakespeare." Some decades earlier another allegory and a literary essay had also suggested in veiled terms that the author of Shakespeare's works was not who he seemed to be. Even as Will Shakspere was being immortalized as the Divine Bard in the 1700s, vague doubts about his credentials seem to have been percolating below the surface.[2]

In the same decade that saw Adams and Jefferson visit Stratford, the Rev. James Wilmot, who lived nearby, was nearing the end of his search for information about Will Shakspere. His conclusion: Will Shakspere did not write the works of Shakespeare; the true author was probably Sir Francis Bacon. Bacon was the most renowned philosopher/essayist of Elizabethan times. Wilmot, a graduate of Oxford, considered his doubts so dangerous, however, that he published nothing and directed that his notes be burned upon his death. His work survives only because he had confided to a friend, who reported on it in confidence to a literary society twenty years later. The literary society kept the confidence, and its papers remained undiscovered until long after others had taken up the authorship question independently.[3]

Not before the first half of the nineteenth century did serious doubts begin to appear in public print about the credentials of Will Shakspere as author. Benjamin Disraeli, the British prime minister, seems to have been the first. In a novel he had a character, probably based on the poet Byron, question whether Shakespeare ever wrote a whole play. "I doubt it," says the character, who goes on to suggest that Shakespeare was just "a botcher-up of old plays." An American lawyer, diplomat, and yachtsman, Joseph C. Hart, published a book on his sailing voyages in which he rails at length against the conventional attribution of the works to Will Shakspere of Stratford. "It is a fraud upon the world to thrust his surreptitious fame upon us," he declares.

By the mid-nineteenth century, established authors and literary critics had begun openly to express their uncertainties and doubts. There was no precipitating event, but rather an under-current of doubt that broke through to the surface here and there. Articles and books on Shakespeare began to appear with titles such as "Who Wrote Shakespeare?" and "Bacon and Shakespeare." Soon the search for the "true author" was launched in earnest. By 1884 more than 250 titles were in print. Sir Francis Bacon remained the leading candidate for several decades, and his interest in anagrams and cryptograms led Baconians to use cryptography to try to prove that he left clues to his authorship in his works. Cryptography became quite a vogue, but the methodology has now been discredited, and Bacon is no longer taken seriously as a possible author of Shakespeare's works.

Ultimately, almost sixty different men, women, and groups of men and women would be proposed as the author(s) of the works of Shakespeare. They ranged from Queen Elizabeth I herself to the Jesuits. They included Christopher Marlowe, the fifth earl of Rutland, and the sixth earl of Derby, who, along with Bacon, were the most prominent candidates until the seventeenth earl of Oxford was proposed in 1920.

The conventional attribution to the man from Stratford was questioned by leading figures in nineteenth-century American literature, including John Greenleaf Whittier, Ralph Waldo Emerson, Walt Whitman, Henry James, and Mark Twain.[4]

Whittier wrote: "Whether Bacon wrote the wonderful plays or not, I am quite sure the man Shakspere [*sic*] neither did nor could."

Emerson, while not rejecting Will Shakspere outright as the author, could not reconcile the "jovial actor and manager" with the poet/dramatist. "I can not marry this fact to his verse," Emerson wrote. "Other admirable men have led lives in some sort of keeping with their thought; but this man, in wide contrast."

Whitman, the poet of the common man, nevertheless rejected the commoner from Stratford-on-Avon, saying he was "firm against Shakspere—I mean the Avon man, the actor." He considered Shakespeare's plays "essentially the plays of an aristocracy." Oxfordians credit him with remarkable insight in guessing that the poet/dramatist was probably born a nobleman. In "November Boughs" (1888), Whitman called Shakespeare's history plays the chief puzzle:

> Conceived out of the fullest heat and pulse of European feudalism—personifying in unparalleled ways the medieval aristocracy, its towering spirit of ruthless and gigantic caste, with its own peculiar air and arrogance (no mere imitation)—only one of the "wolfish earls" so plenteous in the plays themselves, or some born descendant and knower, might seem to be the true author of those amazing works, works in some respects greater than anything else in recorded literature.

Henry James spun his skepticism into a short story, "The Birthplace," in which an older couple, employed as guides at the birthplace of an unnamed playwright, find themselves turned into cynical skeptics who must tell the tourists what they want to hear about the playwright even if there is no truth to it. Shortly after writing the story James said in a letter: "I am 'a sort of' haunted by the conviction that the divine William is the biggest and most successful fraud ever practiced on a patient world."

Mark Twain's interest in the authorship question spanned half a century. It began when he was an apprentice pilot on Mississippi riverboats. He had read a book by Delia Bacon that had widespread influence, and he used her arguments to goad into debate a disputatious master pilot who had a passion for Shakespeare but was ferociously loyal to the Stratford man. They discussed and argued for weeks while piloting boats up and down the Mississippi. The debates served to confirm Twain in his position: "I only *believed* [Sir Francis] Bacon wrote Shakespeare, whereas I *knew* Shakespeare didn't."

Shortly before his death in 1909 Twain wrote *Is Shakespeare Dead? From My Autobiography*, the last book of his lifetime and one he published himself. In it he recounts his debates with the master pilot and his conviction that Will Shakspere did not write the plays and poems of Shakespeare.

In his usual rambling fashion Twain makes three main points: Nothing literary about Will Shakspere in his lifetime has been

found; his death went totally unnoticed; and lawyers find extensive, accurate, and subtle references to the law throughout the
poems and plays. Twain quoted lawyers on Shakespeare's keen
knowledge of the law, and drew a parallel with riverboat piloting. Twain considered it impossible for someone not a pilot to
write about it without making mistakes, even if he read books
about piloting. As Twain put it:

> A man can't handle glibly and easily and comfortably and
> successfully the argot of a trade at which he has not per-
> sonally served. He will make mistakes; he will not, and
> cannot, get the trade-phrasings precisely and exactly right;
> and the moment he departs, by even a shade, from a com-
> mon trade-form, the reader who served that trade will
> know the writer *hasn't*.[5]

Throughout the latter half of the nineteenth century and into
the early twentieth century, establishment scholars, found
mainly in the newly formed English departments at universities,
continued to teach the firmly entrenched belief that the man
from Stratford was the author Shakespeare. Faced with some
sixty candidates for authorship, the professors and lecturers in
the universities and their publishers prudently stayed with the
man from Stratford. In dismissing the other candidates, they also
dismissed the possibility that Will Shakspere might not have
been the poet/dramatist. To accept that possibility would have
meant scrapping nearly a century of scholarship. Scholarly reputations, careers in academia, and even their families' livelihoods
had been built on traditional Shakespearean scholarship, which
assumed that Will Shakspere was the author. Understandably,
the heirs of traditional Stratfordian scholarship were loath to reject or question their inheritance. Will Shakspere remained on
his pedestal.

The extremes diverged. Stratfordian Bardolatry held academia
in its grip. Dissenters were going off on wild tangents with new
candidates for authorship almost yearly. Battle lines were drawn.
Positions became entrenched. Emotions ran high.

Completely overlooked in the scramble to find the true author
was Edward de Vere, seventeenth earl of Oxford. The credit for

proposing him goes to a schoolmaster in northern England, J. Thomas Looney.[6] In 1920 he published *"Shakespeare" Identified in Edward de Vere, the Seventeenth Earl of Oxford.* Looney had taught *The Merchant of Venice* to class after class of students. As a result, he felt he had developed a close understanding of the author's mind and outlook on life. He also had read widely, including books on the authorship question, and was a follower of August Comte, the founder of logical positivism, an approach to general problem solving using scientific methods.

Looney was nothing if not methodical. Instead of plunging into the records of Shakespeare's contemporaries to find a likely suspect, he began by assuming for working purposes that the author was unknown. He then reread all of Shakespeare. Based on his study of the poems and plays and of the commentaries by Shakespearean scholars, he drew up two lists of characteristics that should be found in the author of the works of Shakespeare.

For his profile of the author, Looney first identified the general characteristics he thought the author should have. These were superior education, maturity, recognized genius, intense sensitivity, recognized talent for lyric poetry, apparent eccentricity, and enthusiasm for the theater. He then drew up a list of the more specific characteristics that he found the author should have. These included an aristocratic background with feudal connections, doubts about women, improvidence in money matters, and enthusiasms for Italy, music, and sport, especially falconry.

He began his search by studying lyric poets who used the stanza form of Shakespeare's *Venus and Adonis.* Not long into his research, he came across a poem by Edward de Vere, seventeenth earl of Oxford, that used the same stanza form.

He then looked up Oxford in standard reference books, and he found a match. *The Dictionary of National Biography's* entry on Oxford describes him as an aristocrat with a violent and perverse temper, eccentric taste in dress, recklessness in his waste of substance, and genuine taste in music. He was a patron of acting companies, and he was a writer who had a reputation as one of the best playwrights and courtier poets, although no plays survived, and only some early poems. Ironically, the biography of

Oxford had been written by a confirmed Stratfordian who had also written the biography of Shakespeare, that is, Will Shakspere, for *The Dictionary of National Biography*.

"Shakespeare" Identified, published only in England until 1949, received slight notice. Academics, confirmed in their belief in the Stratford man as the poet/dramatist, noted the author's funny name and dismissed his arguments. Oxford, after all, was just number fifty-nine among the claimants, or whatever the count might have been at the time. A few reviewers praised the book, but sales were never large.

Professor Frederick Tabor Cooper of Columbia University did welcome the book. He said that "every right-minded scholar who seriously cares for the welfare of letters in the larger sense should face the problem that this book presents and argue it to a finish." Sigmund Freud read *"Shakespeare" Identified* and became convinced. He wrote in his *Autobiographical Study*:

> The name "William Shakespeare" is most probably a pseudonym behind which there lies concealed a great unknown, Edward de Vere, Earl of Oxford, a man who has been regarded as the author of Shakespeare's works, [a man who] lost a beloved and admired father while he was still a boy, and completely repudiated his mother, who contracted a new marriage soon after her husband's death.

The novelist John Galsworthy called Looney's book the best detective story he had ever read. He recommended it to his friends and supplied them with copies.[7]

The debate continued on the margins of Shakespearean textual studies. Conventional scholarship produced thousands of books and articles, all based on the assumption that Will Shakspere was the author. Biographers embellished the story of the Stratford man, shaping the story and becoming even more assured in their accounts of his life. The introductions to Shakespeare's works invariably summarized their work. Only occasionally did a Shakespeare professor comment on the authorship controversy, and then usually to dismiss it.

Independent Oxfordian scholars continued to build on the case first laid out in *"Shakespeare" Identified* in 1920. The leading figures have included Bernard M. Ward, Eva Turner Clark, Charles Wisner Barrell, Dorothy Ogburn and Charlton Ogburn, Sr., Charlton Ogburn, and Ruth Loyd Miller. Ward led off with the first fully researched, full-length biography of Oxford. Published in 1928, it remains the standard biography for scholars of all persuasions. Although Ward accepted the case for Oxford's authorship of Shakespeare, his publisher persuaded him to exclude any mention of it from the biography. Ward left it to others to delineate the striking parallels between Oxford's life and the works of Shakespeare, particularly in *Hamlet*.[8] Out of print for many years, Ward's biography has been made available in photocopy by Miller, who has also republished Looney's book and many articles, including her own, on the case for Oxford.

In 1984 Charlton Ogburn relaunched the campaign to have Oxford recognized as the man behind the name Shakespeare. His major work, *The Mysterious William Shakespeare: The Myth and the Reality*, received a number of favorable reviews and became the bible for new Oxfordians. Ogburn was carrying on the work of his parents, who had also been staunch Oxfordians. In 1952 they published a 1,297-page book, *This Star of England*, telling the story of Oxford's life and describing hundreds of references and allusions to his life and times that they found in Shakespeare's poems and plays.

Ogburn, a former State Department official, has written more than a dozen books and many magazine articles on a variety of subjects. In his 892-page book on Oxford as Shakespeare, he strengthens the case for Oxford and deals with objections to it from Stratfordian professors. With its publication he became the leading spokesperson for the Oxfordian cause, and he has appeared on several television programs. In the late twentieth century Ogburn's book has probably been the single most important factor in the growing support for Edward de Vere, seventeenth earl of Oxford, as the poet/dramatist.

Chapter Seven

Oxford's Literary Life

Three days after his father's funeral, twelve-year-old Edward de Vere rode into London, where he was to be a ward of the Crown until he turned twenty-one. The boy arrived from his ancestral home north of London late in the afternoon at the head of an entourage of 140 men on horseback, all in mourning black. He was now the earl of Oxford, the seventeenth in the line of earls, a title he inherited from his father along with the title of lord great chamberlain in the court of Queen Elizabeth I.[1]

His destination was the mansion of William Cecil, a commoner but Queen Elizabeth's master of the court of wards as well as her most influential adviser. Cecil House in the Strand, not far from Charing Cross, became Oxford's new home, where he continued to study with tutors while growing up with Cecil's children.

Cecil's daughter, Anne, was six years old when the new earl of Oxford joined the household. Nine years later they were married. Several months before the wedding, the queen elevated Cecil to the peerage as Lord Burghley. If Lord Burghley is caricatured as Polonius in *Hamlet*—as has long been held by traditional scholarship—then his daughter, Anne, becomes Ophelia, the daughter of Polonius in the play, and Oxford becomes Hamlet.

Oxford led just such a life as might be expected of the author of Shakespeare's works. He was a poet, playwright, and at times a favorite in the queen's court. He traveled in France and Italy. He was a patron of actors and writers. His contemporaries recognized his skill in poetry and drama, although no plays under his name survive. In the last decade of his life, he retired to a mansion near the London suburb of Stratford (not the one on the River Avon). There, he presumably continued to work on his writings until his death in 1604 at the age of fifty-four. His last decade coincided roughly with the decade that saw the greatest production of Shakespeare's poems and plays.

Edward de Vere was born on April 12, 1550, in Castle Hedingham, about forty miles north of London. His birth day was in the same month as Will Shakspere's, but fourteen years earlier. His father, the sixteenth earl of Oxford, an avid sportsman and hunter, held vast properties in southeast England. He traced his lineage back five hundred years to William the Conqueror. Exploits of his ancestors included a command at the battle of Agincourt, the setting for much of Shakespeare's *Henry V*. He also maintained an acting company, which produced plays and masques for his family and friends. When Edward was eleven years old, young Queen Elizabeth, who was to play such an important role in his life, visited Castle Hedingham with her entourage for almost a week.

Edward's father died the following year. Although his mother was still living, as an underage heir to great estates Oxford left his family and became a ward of the Crown. His guardian was William Cecil, later created Lord Burghley, who was empowered to control Oxford's inherited estates on behalf of the queen until Oxford attained his majority at age twenty-one.[2] Cecil was already one of the most powerful men in England. He would become the queen's most constant and influential adviser for the rest of his life and virtually her entire reign, serving as her secretary, treasurer, and chief minister.

At Burghley's mansion Oxford continued to work with tutors. One of them probably was his uncle, Arthur Golding, the translator of Ovid's *Metamorphoses*, which is recognized by all scholars as having had a major influence on Shakespeare's poems and plays. After graduating from Cambridge and then Oxford, he studied law at Gray's Inn, which, as it happens, was noted for its amateur theatricals.

While still in his teens, Oxford killed a cook in Burghley's household with a sword. The incident led some biographers to describe Oxford as a headstrong, unruly youth, quick to reach for his sword. But the record is not clear on who reached first, or what happened. Burghley at first implied it was the cook's fault, but then called it self-defense. Swordplay turns up again in records a dozen years later, when Oxford was reported to have engaged in a "fray," wounding his attacker and himself receiving a wound.[3]

When he reached the age of twenty-one and took his seat in the House of Lords, Oxford was married to Anne Cecil. After an unexplained postponement from September to December, the wedding ceremony took place in Westminster Abbey and was attended by the queen. Although the bride and groom had grown up together at Cecil House, it is not certain that this was a marriage of youthful romance. They were married for more than three years before Anne's first child was born, and even then rumors were widespread that Oxford was not the father.

During his twenties Oxford was active in court circles, saw military action for the first time, traveled to the Continent, and began publishing his first works of prose and poetry. He was at the height of favor with Queen Elizabeth, who always kept her courtiers busy amusing her with music, dancing, banqueting, theatrical works, jousting tournaments, and other entertainments.[4] Elizabeth loved energetic dancing, and Oxford seems to have been one of her favorites. She once sent for him to dance at court, but he refused to dance before visiting Frenchmen. For a sound-and-light show staged for her at Warwick Castle on the River Avon, he was a commander in a mock battle involving hundreds of soldiers. Cannons lofted firebombs across the river a few miles from Stratford-on-Avon. The queen also presided at jousting tournaments; Oxford, an accomplished athlete, took top honors in all three tournaments he is on record as having entered.

Also a tennis player, Oxford is often cited as the antagonist to Sir Philip Sidney in the Great Tennis Court Quarrel. The two were literary rivals, and Sidney had been proposed as a husband for Anne Cecil before she married Oxford. The two quarreled over tennis court privileges before a number of distinguished spectators. Sidney said Oxford called him a "puppy," ordering him to leave, which he did. The queen had to mediate and persuade Sidney to apologize to the earl. Biographies of Sidney blame Oxford for the quarrel. Oxford's twentieth-century biographer, Bernard M. Ward, however, demonstrates that Sidney probably was in the wrong.

Oxford's first experience of actual warfare occurred when he was twenty years old. He was attached to the commander of the queen's forces that suppressed a rebellion on the border with Scotland. The suppression has been described as brutal. Towns were seized and burned. At least two fortresses came under siege. Hundreds of men were taken from their homes and executed. No records, however, tell where Oxford was during the campaign.

Apparently eager for travel and adventure, Oxford slipped out of England without the queen's approval and turned up in Brussels, but was called home. He was more successful the next year, his twenty-fourth, when he secured the permission of the queen to travel on the Continent. For sixteen months he toured France and Italy, stopping in Paris, Padua, Venice, Siena, Sicily, and probably Rome, On his way home his ship was attacked by pirates and he lost all his belongings.

On his return he found himself in the midst of a paternity scandal. His wife had given birth while he was on the continent, but rumors were spread about the date of birth and whether he was the father. His wife's physician reported that Oxford had said he could not be the father, but the circumstances of the report cast doubt on its validity. Whatever happened, Oxford refused to have anything to do with his wife or her father, and for several years was estranged from her.

In his early twenties Oxford's prose and poetry began to appear under his own name, his initials, or pseudonyms. His work included a number of lyric poems and two prefaces to translations from the Italian and the Latin. One translation was a book on the ideal courtier, the other a philosophy of life. His contemporaries praised his poetic talent. Ward, a judicious biographer, says they "accounted him a renowned poet, a pioneer in literature, and a keen patron of men of letters." About two dozen of Oxford's poems survive. The number is approximate because some attributions are disputed.[5]

Oxford was an active patron of writers, and a number of them dedicated their works to him, sometimes in terms that indicate that he was directing their work. He began his long association with a group of poets and playwrights when he was in his late twenties. Two of its members were Robert Greene, whose name was attached to *Groatsworth* much later, and John Lyly, who dedicated the second part of his book, *Euphues*, to Oxford. For at least a decade, Lyly, also a playwright, was Oxford's private secretary and probably the general manager of his acting companies.[6]

In his thirties Oxford acquired a mistress, several acting companies, more military experience, and an enormous annual stipend from Queen Elizabeth.[7] The decade, however, started off disastrously. While estranged from his wife, Oxford started an affair with a court beauty, Anne Vavasor, who was not yet twenty years old. The affair resulted in the birth of a son and almost three months' detention in the Tower of London, on orders of Queen Elizabeth, not just for the father but for the young mother and probably her illegitimate infant, too. Anne Vavasor was one of the queen's maids of honor; Oxford had been in high favor with the queen. The queen, always angered by dalliances with her maids of honor, was not pleased. Other repercussions followed. Oxford and Anne Vavasor's cousin fought in public and both were wounded, Oxford more seriously. Over the next year there occurred several street melees in which two of Oxford's men and one of his rival's men were slain.

A portrait of Anne Vavasor shows a slender, dark-haired woman with dark eyes, leading some Oxfordians to surmise that she was the Dark Lady of Shakespeare's *Sonnets*. The affair lasted a few years, and then Oxford returned to his marriage.

His wife, Anne, bore him four more children over the next five years. Their youngest daughter, Susan, was married to one of the two brothers addressed in the dedication of the *First Folio* of Shakespeare's plays. Another daughter had been proposed as a bride for the other brother. The third daughter married the sixth earl of Derby, who reportedly was interested in playwriting.

Oxford's three experiences of battle were brief, and no word remains about what specific action he saw. During the Scots border rebellion he had been attached briefly to the commander. During the war between the Protestants and the Spanish Catholics in the Low Countries, he was one of the commanders of the expeditionary force, but was recalled after less than two months, perhaps the result of court intrigue. Dutch pirates attacked the ship carrying his belongings and made off with them. When Spain sent its famed Armada against England in 1588, Oxford outfitted a ship and joined the British fleet that ultimately defeated the Spanish and their hopes to invade England. Oxford himself apparently left the fleet before the decisive sea battle to join the queen and her army at Tilbury.

When he was thirty Oxford revived the family tradition of maintaining an acting company, and he leased the First Blackfriars theater. John Lyly, his private secretary, produced plays there that were then performed for Queen Elizabeth and her court. The records also associate Lyly with other acting companies in the decade that followed.

Oxford's eminence among writers of the time was described by two contemporaries, and one of them noted that Oxford's writings did not appear under his own name. William Webbe in *A Discourse of English Poetry* commended the poetic skills of the lords and gentlemen in the queen's court and concluded that Oxford could claim to be "the most excellent among the rest." The author of *The Art of English Poesy* agreed, and added that he knew courtiers who wrote well but suppressed it "or else suffered it to be published without their own names to it, as if it were a discredit for a gentleman to seem learned and to show himself amorous of any good art." Later, the author noted that some noblemen "have written excellently well, as it would appear if their doings could be found out and made public with the rest, of which number is first that noble gentleman Edward, Earl of Oxford."[8]

Oxford was not so skillful, however, in his financial affairs. When he was a ward, Lord Burghley controlled his assets, and

Burghley's integrity has been questioned. Oxfordian scholars conclude that Burghley, who amassed a great fortune during his career, manipulated the finances of his young, wealthy wards, even after they reached the age of twenty-one. Over the years, Oxford's land and estates were sold to raise money. Historians generally characterize him as improvident and a spendthrift because he seemed to be chronically short of cash, although there is no evidence of extravagant expenditures. When he was thirty-six, however, his financial problems were solved. The queen authorized a grant of one thousand pounds a year for life, paid quarterly from the state treasury, with no strings attached.

One thousand pounds was an extraordinary sum. Money-value comparisons are difficult to make, but it is generally held to be the equivalent of several hundred thousand dollars in the late twentieth century. No reason for the grant was given by the queen, who expressly directed that no accounting of it should be required. No public service by Oxford could explain the grant; he held no position of great authority or command in the queen's government. The records do not show that he was particularly active in Elizabeth's court. Possibly she was simply maintaining Oxford's income at a level required by an earl who was a leading nobleman in her court. Biographer Ward considers and dismisses that possibility, noting that Elizabeth was notoriously tightfisted with money.[9]

Ward and most Oxfordians conclude that the queen was probably reimbursing Oxford, one of her favorite courtiers, for his work with the acting companies. She was famous for her love of literature and theatrical entertainments. If so, Queen Elizabeth would thus have been a major patron of the theater, with Oxford as her intermediary and one of the principal playwrights, although which plays were his was never openly acknowledged.

An idea of Oxford's appearance and manner can be glimpsed here and there in the records, which include two painted portraits. One of them, which carries Oxford's name behind and above his head, is the portrait of a nobleman about forty years old. He has auburn hair, arching eyebrows, a Roman nose, carefully trimmed moustache and short beard, and what might be described as sensitive lips. They seem pursed as if about to whistle. The rightward glance of the eyes is austere, almost imperious. Around his neck hangs a ribbon holding a boar, the crest of the de Vere family. In an earlier portrait, a copy of one he sent to his wife from Paris when he was twenty-five, the eyebrows are much thinner and farther apart, the moustache almost pencil-thin, and the chin clean-shaven.[10]

Oxford apparently dressed in the latest fashion. Queen Elizabeth's court was famous for the extravagant attire concocted by her courtiers. Oxford, upon his return from Italy, introduced new fashions, including perfumed gloves, and new mannerisms that drew sarcastic verses from a scholarly pedant named Gabriel Harvey, who later apologized.

A flattering image of Oxford was drawn by George Chapman, a playwright, a respected man of letters, and the translator of Homer. In one of his plays Chapman gave a character the following speech:

> I overtook, coming from Italy,
> In Germany, a great and famous Earl
> Of England; the most goodly fashion'd man
> I ever saw: from head to foot in form
> Rare and most absolute; he had a face
> Like one of the most ancient honor'd Romans
> From whence his noblest family was deriv'd;
> He was beside of spirit passing great,
> Valiant and learn'd, and liberal as the sun,
> Spoke and writ sweetly, or of learned subjects,
> Or of the discipline of public weals;
> And 'twas the Earl of Oxford.

In his early forties Oxford, a widower for three years, married his second wife, Elizabeth Trentham, the daughter of a landowner and one of the queen's maids of honor. A son, Henry, who became the eighteenth earl of Oxford, was the only child of his second marriage. A few years later the couple moved to Hackney, near Stratford, the suburb north of London.

When Oxford was forty-eight, he was specifically identified by

Edward de Vere, seventeenth earl of Oxford

1550 Born April 12 at Castle Hedingham, in Essex.

1562 His father dies; he becomes a ward of Burghley.

1564 Receives degree from Cambridge University. (Will Shakespeare is born in Stratford-on-Avon.)

1566 Receives Master's Degree from Oxford University.

1567 Admitted to Gray's Inn law school.

1570 Joins a military campaign on the Scotland border.

1571 Marries Burghley's daughter.

1575 Begins a 16-month trip to France and Italy.

1578 Praised as an excellent poet and prolific writer.

1577–86 Is often cited as a patron of literature; is the patron of two companies of actors.

1581 Confined to the Tower of London in a political dispute; again for affair with an attendant to the queen.

1582 Injured in street fighting over his affair.

1586 Queen grants him 1,000 pounds a year.

1589 Described as a writer who doesn't sign his works.

1590s The sonnets are probably written.

1592 A widower, he marries his second wife.

1593 *Venus and Adonis* is published; first appearance of the name William Shakespeare.

1593–1604 Years of greatest output of Shakespeare's plays, most of them anonymously.

1598 *Love's Labor's Lost* first play with Shakespeare's name on it; Meres lists Oxford as a playwright.

1603 Queen Elizabeth dies.

1604 Oxford dies.

1609 *Shake-speares Sonnets*, with hints author is dead.

(1616 Shakspere of Stratford dies, without eulogies.)

1623 The *First Folio*, the collected plays of Shakespeare, with a dedication to Oxford's son-in-law.

name as a playwright for the first and last time during his life-time, as far as any records show. None of his plays were named. The identification came in Francis Meres's *Palladis Tamia*, where Oxford's name was first in a list of seventeen playwrights whom Meres deemed "best for comedy." This was the same common-place book that first named Shakespeare as a playwright and provided a list of twelve plays by him.

During his forties and up to his death at fifty-four, Oxford's name appears infrequently in the historical records that have been turned up so far. Those who hold that he was the man behind the pseudonym Shakespeare suggest that he had retired from public life and the court to revise and expand the early plays, write new ones, and add to the sonnets. These were the years when most of the plays by Shakespeare appeared and were performed, according to conventional chronology. (Will Shak-spere was in his late twenties and his thirties.)

One of the historical records provides a poignant convergence of history and literature. It names Oxford, fifty-one, as the senior nobleman sitting in judgment in the treason trial of the earl of Essex and the third earl of Southampton—the same Southamp-ton to whom Shakespeare had dedicated his two long narrative poems, *Venus and Adonis* and *The Rape of Lucrece*, less than a decade earlier. And the same Southampton who had been sought as a husband for Oxford's daughter. Both defendants were found guilty. Essex was beheaded. Southampton was sen-tenced to life in prison. Two years later, James I, in his first act as king, freed Southampton.

The treason trial was the second for Oxford. Fifteen years ear-lier, he had been one of the commissioners in the trial of Mary Queen of Scots, Queen Elizabeth's cousin. Mary conducted her own defense, which was said to be eloquent. Oxfordians find similarities between her plea for mercy and Portia's speech, which begins, "The quality of mercy is not strained," in *The Mer-chant of Venice*.

King James I, who was Mary's son, was an enthusiastic sup-porter of the theater. He, his wife, and their son became the patrons of three acting companies. In one of his first acts as king, James continued Oxford's grant of one thousand pounds a year, and appointed him to the Privy Council. Reportedly, he also ordered that seven plays by Shakespeare be performed at court in his first Christmas season in London.

Oxford died at Hackney on June 24, 1604, the year following Queen Elizabeth's death. "The plague" is noted in the margin of his burial record. Oxford's final resting place is shrouded in mystery. His widow specified that she wanted to be buried next to him in the church at Hackney, but there are no records of a tomb or monument there; and the church itself was destroyed in 1798. Several years after Oxford's death, a son of Arthur Golding, Oxford's uncle, wrote in a family history that Oxford "lieth buried at Westminster." There is no record of it, however, in the records or on the grave markers of Westminster Abbey, although Oxford's first wife and other members of his family were buried there.[11]

Oxford's surviving daughters, Susan in particular, provide a significant linkage between Oxford, an acclaimed playwright with no plays attributed to his name, and the collected plays of Shakespeare published in the *First Folio*. The year after Oxford died, Susan, his youngest daughter, then seventeen, married into the Herbert family. The Herberts were generous patrons of Ben Jonson, who became the impresario of the *First Folio*. And eighteen years after Oxford's death, the two Herbert brothers, one of them Susan's husband, were the earls to whom the *First Folio* was dedicated. The brothers were Philip Herbert, Susan's husband, and William Herbert, who were the earls of Montgomery and Pembroke, respectively. As wealthy men, they may well have financed publication of the *First Folio*, one of the most expensive printing undertakings of the time.[12]

Susan and her sister Elizabeth were closely associated with Ben Jonson, too. His book of poetic epigrams included one addressed to Susan, and the book itself was dedicated to her brother-in-law. Both Susan and Elizabeth appeared in court entertainments, called masques, that were written by Ben Jonson. In these masques, based on classical themes, members of the royal family and the court took roles on stage in elaborate costumes.

Elizabeth's husband was also connected with the theater and with her father. Her husband was William Stanley, sixth earl of Derby, who was Oxford's friend in his later years. Derby was

also a patron of acting companies and reportedly wrote comedies, although no plays by him are known. In the early twentieth
century he was one of the three or four leading candidates
thought to have been the author of Shakespeare's works. Some
Oxfordians think he may have been a collaborator with Oxford
on some of the later plays.

The third of Oxford's three daughters, Bridget, was at one time
sought in marriage for the second of the two Herbert brothers,
William. If she had married him, two of Oxford's daughters
would have been married to the two brothers to whom the *First
Folio* was dedicated. She was only thirteen and he was seventeen
when the Herberts tried to arrange the marriage. For whatever
reason the marriage did not occur.

William Herbert grew up to become the third earl of Pembroke, Susan's brother-in-law, and the most influential of the extended family in the publication of the *First Folio*. He won the
position of lord chamberlain, the senior official in charge of court
entertainments and the public theater, including publication of
plays. He had actively sought the position and once he gained
it he declined several times to give it up for higher office. While
in the position he arranged for a generous annual payment to
Ben Jonson, and in the year that work began on printing the *First
Folio* he increased the payments temporarily to two hundred
pounds a year, about ten to twenty times the annual salary of a
schoolteacher in a town like Stratford-on-Avon.

Thus, the two Herbert brothers, to whom the *First Folio* of
Shakespeare's plays were dedicated, were closely linked to Oxford's three surviving daughters by marriage, by theatrical interests, and by close association with Ben Jonson. If Oxford's
daughters had wanted to assure the publication of Shakespeare's
plays, Susan's brother-in-law, as lord chamberlain, was in the
perfect position to do just that. And he had made sure he was
in the position for the time required to make it happen. The
Herberts even arranged for a Herbert cousin to be named master
of the revels, the administrative official directly overseeing the
theaters, acting companies, and publication of plays.

The facts of Oxford's life as poet, playwright, and patron of
acting companies and the connections between his daughters
and the *First Folio* make a strong case for him as the true author.

The case is reinforced by an analysis of how his life is reflected in Shakespeare's works, especially *Hamlet*, and how his life span makes a better fit with the estimated dates of composition of Shakespeare's works.

Chapter Eight

The Case for Oxford as Author

On a Friday morning in September 1987 three justices of the Supreme Court of the United States sat in judgment on the Oxford challenge to the Bard of Avon. The moot court was held in a Methodist church in Washington, DC, before an audience of about a thousand. The case for the Bard of Avon and the case for the earl of Oxford were in the hands of two law professors.

The decision that day went against Oxford, although two of the justices expressed lingering doubts. But that was not the end of it. The following year, a similar moot court was held in London before three law lords of Great Britain. The verdict was the same; they voted in favor of Will Shakspere and against Oxford. But that still was not the end of it.[1]

Since then, two of the three justices of the U.S. Supreme Court have declared they now doubt that Will Shakspere was the author. One of them, Justice Harry A. Blackmun, wrote to Charlton Ogburn:

> The Oxfordians have presented a very strong—almost fully convincing—case for their point of view. The debate continues and it is well that it does. We need this enlightenment in these otherwise somewhat dismal days. If I had to

rule on the evidence presented, it would be in favor of the Oxfordians.

A second justice, John Paul Stevens, admitted later in a lecture that he had "lingering doubts and gnawing uncertainties" about Will Shakspere's purported authorship. In a law review article, he used the case of Lord Oxford versus Will Shakspere to illustrate his views on the canons of statutory construction. The case for Oxford was put most persuasively in the article.

Another Supreme Court justice, Lewis F. Powell, Jr., who did not participate in the moot court, has also expressed his skepticism. He wrote to Ogburn that he never thought the man of Stratford-on-Avon wrote the plays of Shakespeare.[2]

That four Supreme Court justices should evince such keen interest in the controversy and such extensive knowledge about the arguments for both sides is eloquent testimony to the validity and significance of the debate. Their interest suggests that Stratfordians who dismiss the Oxford challenge as unfounded and unworthy even of consideration should rethink their reluctance to address the issue. The case for Edward de Vere, seventeenth earl of Oxford, himself a lawyer, is most persuasive for many who listen to and weigh the arguments for both sides, as they might do if they were sitting in judgment in a moot court.

Literary figures, as well as lawyers, have been impressed by the case for Oxford. They include David McCullough, the author of *Truman*; essayist and novelist Wilfrid Sheed; literary editor Clifton Fadiman; and novelists Hamilton Basso and John Galsworthy. Sigmund Freud, who took a keen interest in literature and especially Shakespeare, wrote to J. Thomas Looney that he was convinced by Looney's book that Oxford wrote Shakespeare.[3]

Oxford's life fits Shakespeare. Without exception, the events and concerns of his life are just what would be expected in the life of an Elizabethan who wrote the works of Shakespeare. This is true in general and in the particulars of his life.

Oxford was born into the nobility and was a major figure for years in the court of Queen Elizabeth. Shakespeare's plays were written from an aristocratic point of view.[4] With few exceptions, the author's voice is heard through kings, queens, dukes, princes, earls, countesses, and others who are born to royalty or nobility. Commoners are mostly buffoons and louts, with names like Bottom, Snout, Dogberry, Elbow, and Sly, and are usually objects of ridicule. They are seen through the eyes of an aristocrat.[5]

All the plays but one (*The Merry Wives of Windsor*) focus on the character and troubles of royal or nobly born personages whose manners and motives are plumbed to the depths. Even *Merry Wives* is set near one of the queen's country properties, Windsor Castle. Oxford probably knew the neighborhood quite well from visits by the court there. The language of the plays, regal and sophisticated, is that of the aristocrats of Cambridge, Oxford, and London. (Will Shakspere would have had to pick up the ways of the court and nobility by extended observation from the outside; he also would have had to shed his Warwickshire accent and dialect by his early twenties to become the consummate master of the English language as spoken by the well-educated literati of London.)

No one would argue that Shakespeare necessarily had to have been an aristocrat to write about royalty. Other Elizabethan poets wrote about royalty, too. None, however, was able to do it with the total authority and conviction of Shakespeare. In fact, even a stalwart Stratfordian like Professor Northrop Frye recognizes that "Shakespeare seems to have had the instincts of a born courtier." Oxford, of course, was a born courtier.[6]

A contemporary poem by John Davies also seems to say that Shakespeare, whoever he was, was a nobleman. Davies's short, enigmatic epigram was addressed "To our English Terence, Mr. Will Shake-speare." In it Davies says that if Shakespeare had not played some kingly parts in sport, he would have been a companion for a king. The poem is rarely even mentioned in conventional scholarship, although it is one of the few that refer to Shakespeare as an actual person. Stratfordian scholars generally offer no other reading of the lines, which seem to eliminate Will Shakspere, the commoner, as the actor/dramatist.[7]

Some Oxfordians take the poem as alluding to Oxford, under the pseudonym Shakespeare, risking his position at court by consorting with lowly actors. In addition, the reference to the Roman playwright Terence in the title may have special significance if

Will Shakspere was the decoy author for Oxford. Terence was a freed slave and writer who was generally believed to have been a decoy author for Roman playwrights of rank.

Oxford studied the classics at Oxford and Cambridge universities and with tutors who were notable scholars; he spoke and wrote in Latin and French, and he knew Italian and probably some Greek and Hebrew. Shakespeare's works show an extensive knowledge of the ancient authors and an easy familiarity with Latin and French. A whole scene in *Henry V* is entirely in idiomatic French.

Many of the plays and poems have classical themes. *The Comedy of Errors*, one of the earliest works, is based on a play by Plautus, which Shakespeare seems to have read in the original Latin. Ovid was the inspiration for the two, long narrative poems and for the first tragedy, *Titus Andronicus*.[8] (The debate continues over whether Will Shakspere, from what is known of his life, could have learned classical literature and ancient and modern languages through independent study to the extent they are demonstrated in Shakespeare's works—on top of everything else he was supposed to have been doing in "the Lost Years" of his early twenties.)

Oxford's uncle, Arthur Golding, translated Ovid's *Metamorphoses* from the Latin. Shakespeare drew heavily on Ovid for inspiration. All scholars have recognized the influence that Ovid's book had on Shakespeare, both in the original Latin and in the distinctive translation by Golding, who was a member of Burghley's household, a manager of young Oxford's estates, and probably his tutor. Golding published his racy translation of Ovid's twelve-thousand-line poem in two parts when Oxford was fourteen and seventeen years old. Oxford was perfectly placed to see firsthand and perhaps participate in Golding's translation.[9]

In style as well as subject matter, moreover, the translation of Ovid is unlike Golding's many other translations. *Metamorphoses* celebrates pagan gods and tells mythical tales of physical transformations and amorous adventures. Golding, however, was a devout and stern Puritan who translated John Calvin's sermons and other sober religious tracts. Oxfordians suggest that the racy style and imaginative use of the English language in the translation of Ovid may have been supplied by Oxford, the future

Shakespeare. Well into the twentieth century some critics have considered Golding's translation still the best. Whether or not Oxford had a hand in the translation, all scholars agree that Ovid's *Metamorphoses* as translated by his uncle and mentor was the classical work that had the single most powerful impact on the works of Shakespeare.

Oxford studied law at Gray's Inn, and twice sat as a judge on England's highest tribunals. Shakespeare's plays, according to lawyers who have analyzed them, contain many allusions to the law that are accurate and subtle. Trials figure in more than a quarter of the plays. The references to law are not merely dropped into a play to parade book learning or make a legalistic point; they are part of the flow of Shakespeare's thoughts. More than a dozen books, and many articles, have been written about Shakespeare's knowledge of the law. In the nineteenth century John Campbell, the Lord Chief Justice of Great Britain, wrote that "to Shakespeare's law, lavishly as he expounds it, there can be neither demurrer, nor bill of exceptions nor writ of error."[10]

A notorious line in *Henry VI Part 2* is often quoted out of context as a slam against lawyers by Shakespeare. In fact, it is a compliment. By itself the line sounds derogatory: "The first thing we do let's kill all the lawyers." In the scene, however, it is spoken by one of a mob of would-be rebels led by Jack Cade, a rabble-rouser who would disrupt and overturn the social order to his own advantage. The line, being given to a bad guy, backhandedly recognizes the crucial importance of the law and lawyers in the preservation of social order and the rule of law.

It is not surprising, then, that since the earliest days of Shakespearean scholarship, lawyers have been intrigued by the works of Shakespeare and by the authorship question. Some of the leading editors of Shakespeare's works were trained as lawyers. In the twentieth century, lawyers have been in the forefront of those who hold that Oxford, himself a lawyer, was the author of the works of Shakespeare. Charlton Ogburn, Sr., and Ruth Loyd Miller, leading Oxfordian scholars, were trained in the law and active in its practice. Several books by lawyers have been devoted to the authorship question. In 1961 the American Bar Association published *Shakespeare Cross-Examination*, a collection of articles and letters on the subject that had appeared in the *ABA*

Journal. In the foreword, the editor-in-chief wrote: "The problem is not merely a literary one; the question of the identity of the author of the plays is also one of evidence, and therefore within the province of lawyers."[11]

Oxford traveled on the Continent, particularly in France and Italy. Shakespeare's plays, although written, performed, and published in England, are for the most part set on the Continent. Two-thirds of them are set in France, Italy, or ancient Rome and Greece. Scholars have noted that precise details about towns in northern Italy, especially Venice, demonstrate first-hand knowledge acquired by an observant and retentive visitor. (None of the plays draws on the experiences of a young man from a rural market town who goes to the capital to be an actor and make his fame in the theater. And there is no record that Will Shakspere traveled beyond Stratford and London.)

Oxford was a patron of acting companies and dramatists. During his thirties he maintained two acting companies. Among the dramatists who acknowledged his patronage were John Lyly, for many years his secretary; Robert Greene of *Groatsworth* fame; and Anthony Munday.[12] Shakespeare's sense of what makes dramatic theater is unquestioned. The plays reflect the point of view of a writer-director, not an actor. Hamlet takes charge of the visiting troupe of players who will stage the play within the play; he organizes them, directs them, and provides new lines for them.

Oxford was recognized in his day as an accomplished poet, and as many as two dozen poems survive under his name, initials, or motto, all from his youth. Shakespeare's poetry can be shown to be remarkably similar. Louis P. Benezet, an Oxfordian, devised a challenge to prove it. He put together thirteen different passages of four to eight lines selected from poetry signed by Oxford and poetry signed by Shakespeare. Six passages are Oxfordian, seven Shakespearean. The challenge for Shakespearean scholars is to judge which author, if indeed there were two, wrote which passages, solely on intrinsic literary characteristics. (No fair reading Oxford's poems.) So far, no one is known to have done it successfully, although not many want to try. Of course, the Benezet challenge by itself does not prove Oxford's authorship, but it does show that he could write poetry in his teenage years that was quite Shakespearean. (See appendix D for the Benezet challenge.)

Oxford the mature poet can be seen as a better fit than Will Shakspere as the author of *Venus and Adonis* and *The Rape of Lucrece*. Oxford was forty-four, an experienced poet, playwright, and classicist when they were published. The narrative poems, the first writings to carry Shakespeare's name, are polished, sophisticated works full of classical imagery and rhetorical devices. Both show an easy familiarity with Latin literature. *Venus and Adonis*, taking its inspiration from Ovid's *Metamorphoses*, has nearly twelve hundred lines of sustained poetic imagery. *Lucrece*, with nearly two thousand lines, is based on Ovid and on Livy's history of Rome. They are almost certainly not the first efforts of a budding poet and playwright. (Will Shakspere was twenty-eight when the poems were published, and if he was the author there is not a word about any apprenticeship work before these stunning accomplishments.)

Shakespeare's byline does not appear on the title pages of the two poems, where it would usually be found. Instead, it is on the short dedications. Some Oxfordians suggest that this indicates Oxford's reluctance to use a pseudonym in place of his own name on poems he was proud of having written. Both poems are clear of errors and misprints, evidence that the author read proofs and took care that the poems were well printed. Both were very popular and went through many printings in the decades that followed.

The two poems were dedicated to the third earl of Southampton, who was certainly well known to Oxford throughout his life. Southampton was about nineteen at the time of the dedications and, like Oxford, had been in his teens a ward of Lord Burghley, Oxford's father-in-law. A few years earlier, Burghley had tried to arrange a marriage between his granddaughter, Oxford's oldest daughter, and Southampton. Oxford's daughter, Elizabeth, was then fifteen. The young Southampton refused to go along with the plan.

Despite intensive research, no links between Will Shakspere and Southampton have been found, neither before nor after the dedications.[13] Southampton's patronage would have been valuable for Will Shakspere, who seemed eager for money and status.

But nothing came of it. Nor do the dedications sound like a commoner addressing a nobleman. It's difficult to understand how
he could have gotten away with it. Only by positing a tremendous, undocumented rise in status can scholars explain how a
twenty-nine-year-old, unpublished, unacclaimed commoner
could suddenly address an earl in the gracious and familiar
terms of the dedications. The rigid class system of Elizabethan
times would not have allowed it.

Other correspondences to Oxford's life that are found in the
works of Shakespeare are many and striking. They range from
botany to war. Oxford was a ward in Burghley's household during the years that Burghley employed the leading horticulturist
of the time to mange his extensive gardens. Shakespeare's references to flowers and plants are recognized as accurate and
sensitive. A nineteenth-century botanist counted as many as fifty
different flowers and plants referred to in poetical terms and
another hundred in a more prosaic way.[14]

Oxford saw military action in three armed conflicts. Shakespeare wrote knowledgeably about war and military command.
"It is clear," writes G. B. Harrison, a leading Stratfordian scholar,
"that he had an extraordinary knowledge of soldiers....This intimate knowledge is seen again and again."[15] (Will Shakspere
had no known military record.)

Extensive references and subtle allusions to falconry point to
an aristocratic author; falconry was preeminently a sport of the
aristocracy. Other references in Shakespeare's works—to jousting, hunting, fencing, horsemanship, medicine,[16] music, and
dancing—have all been cited with considerable plausibility as
reinforcing the impression that a well-educated, well-placed aristocrat was the author of the works of William Shakespeare under
that pseudonym, not a self-educated actor from the lower clas-
ses.

How Oxford may have selected "William Shakespeare" as his
pseudonym and what he thought about it are not known, but
there are some suggestive clues to its origin. Before succeeding
to his father's title as earl at age twelve, young Edward de Vere
was viscount Bulbeck and his crest a lion that brandishes a lance,
or shakes a spear. The jousting spear in the crest is broken, indicating a victory with a solid hit on the adversary in the joust.

The name Shake-speare also recalls the Greek goddess Pallas Athena—known as the spear-shaker—who was associated with poetry and the theater. Poets and orators rehearsed their compositions in her temple in ancient Athens, which was known as the Athenaeum. Similar institutions were later established at Rome and Lyon.[17]

Oxford's life fits the life that Shakespeare should have led. Being fourteen years older, Oxford's lifespan (1550–1604) also makes a better fit with the period when Shakespeare's works were appearing and being performed, whereas Will Shakspere's dates (1564–1616) require some force fitting and leave some loose ends in the chronology.

Chapter Nine

Oxford's Life Span and Dating the Plays

In Shakespearean biography, chronology is destiny.

Dating the composition of Shakespeare's works has always been a thorny issue. The difficulties arise because there are no manuscripts, diaries, letters, or other records that tell when the plays and poems were written. To estimate a year of composition, scholars rely on a variety of evidence. Most directly helpful are dates of registry in court records, dates of performances, and dates of publication. Obviously, the plays were written sometime before these dates, perhaps years before. Unfortunately, for many plays these helpful dates are missing. Also significant, but more elusive, are references to the plays by contemporaries, allusions in the plays to contemporary events, and the author's evolving style of writing over the years. Assessing the authenticity of all these variables and weighing their merits have always been major preoccupations of Shakespearean scholars.

The question of when the poems and plays were written bears directly on the question of who wrote them. Stratfordian scholars argue that Oxford died too soon to have written the late plays; *The Tempest* is a favorite example (see chapter 11). For their part, Oxfordian scholars cannot accept that Will Shakspere, if he was the author, would have retired to rusticate in Stratford at the height of his creative powers and success in the theater. More important, they argue that at the start of his supposed career there was not enough time for him to gain the broad experience of life and literature needed to write the early plays.

Shakespeare's first plays were written when Will Shakspere was twenty-four or twenty-five years old, according to leading Stratfordian scholars. That would be just three or four years after his twins were born in Stratford-on-Avon. The *Oxford Shakespeare* gives the first play as *The Two Gentlemen of Verona*, written "probably in the late 1580s." Will Shakspere turned twenty-four in 1588. Bevington suggests *Love's Labour's Lost* as the earliest: "Possibly, then, the play was first written in about 1588–1589." The *Riverside Shakespeare* lists *Henry VI Part 1* as the first play, with a proposed date of composition of 1589–1590.[1]

The three scholarly editions of the collected works of Shakespeare disagree as to which play should be listed as his first. None of them would suggest that all three plays were written in those two years. In fact, each dates the others' selections several years later. They do agree, however, that Shakespeare's first plays were probably written in the years when Will Shakspere was twenty-four and twenty-five years old.[2]

After the first play, whichever one it was, more plays began to appear rapidly at the rate of about two a year, according to Stratfordian chronology. By the time Will Shakspere is twenty-eight, the total reaches seven as proposed by the same three leading Shakespeare editions. The four additional plays are *Richard III*, *The Comedy of Errors*, and the other two *Henry VI* plays. To these seven major plays should be added at least the first of the two, long narrative poems, namely *Venus and Adonis*, which was published when Will Shakspere was twenty-nine, plus perhaps some of the 154 sonnets.

Seven plays by age twenty-eight are also suggested as a possibility by Professor Schoenbaum.[3] But he includes two plays not named by the others; they are *Titus Andronicus* and *The Taming of the Shrew*. If so, he writes, the actor from Stratford would have "experimented, with extraordinary success, in the three dramatic genres—comedy, tragedy and history."

The combined total would then rise to nine plays, plus the narrative poem, by age twenty-eight. Of course, none would accept nine as the total written by that year. Their opinions differ about which plays were written when, and that's understandable. Dating the plays is a hazardous business. The evidence is scant and uncertain. The fact remains, however, that Stratfordian scholarship finds enough reason to date the writing of nine major plays plus *Venus and Adonis* in the four or five years between Will Shakspere's twenty-fourth and twenty-eighth years.

Miracles aside, critics of this Stratfordian dating find it hard to accept that Will Shakspere—from what is known about him—could have instantly excelled in comedy, tragedy, history, and lyric poetry on such a scale in his mid-twenties. The achievement may be within the realm .of possibility, but it seems unlikely in the extreme. Even genius, and Shakespeare was certainly a genius, cannot supply the range of life experience demonstrated in the nine early works as proposed by Stratfordian scholarship.

However many plays were written during Will Shakspere's mid-twenties, those years are his famous "Lost Years." Nothing in the record tells where he was or what he was doing. He himself left no record of his life in the theater. Stratfordian scholars almost never mention his age and inexperience when estimating composition dates of the early plays. They cite only calendar years. This reticence may be a symptom of their unease about how much life experience Will Shakspere would have had to cram into his early twenties.

Non-Stratfordians also ask how Will Shakspere, if he was the author, found time to write the early plays and poems. He was not independently wealthy. Playwriting didn't pay much. He is supposed to have been earning a living and learning his playwriting craft by acting regularly in many different roles. Presumably he was also observing the goings-on at Queen Elizabeth's court and absorbing the ways of royalty and the nobility. He couldn't have had much time left at the end of the day to write poetry and plays by candlelight.

Even more remarkable, even surpassing belief for some, would be the acquisition by a young and supposedly very busy actor newly arrived in London from Stratford of all the classical culture, English history, immense vocabulary,[4] sophisticated language, and knowledge and experience of life that is found in the early plays and poems. Plus Latin, French, Italian, and at least some Greek and Hebrew. How he could have learned enough by his mid-twenties, given his mundane Stratford background, to write about so much so well when so inexperienced is difficult to understand.

If challenged, Stratfordians usually reply: "He was a genius." In the nineteenth century they called it "Divine Inspiration." Literary genius, however, must have raw material to draw upon. The richer and more diverse the content of the writing, the greater the need to draw on diversity and intensity of experience. Unlike music or mathematics, great and sustained writing is the result of genius working on life experience and acquired knowledge, neither of which can be part of the innate gift of genius. Even if endowed retrospectively with a genius that is almost superhuman, Will Shakspere still, according to the records, had precious little time to gain the life experience demonstrated so dramatically in the early plays.

Most people are under the general impression that Shakespeare launched his career in print with his plays. But that's not the way it happened. He burst onto the literary scene from nowhere in 1593 with *Venus and Adonis*, the long, highly sophisticated and polished narrative poem that was Shakespeare's most popular published work among his contemporaries. It was reprinted nine times.[5] (Will Shakspere turned twenty-nine the year it was published.) Before that year, there had been no record of any plays signed by Shakespeare, no mention of that name as a writer, no sign of any apprenticeship work. If Will Shakspere was the ambitious actor and prolific playwright in his twenties, he remained strangely silent and uncelebrated until almost thirty years old.

Venus and Adonis, the first work to carry the name that would become so famous, was followed the next year by *The Rape of Lucrece*, also with a dedication by Shakespeare and also very popular. For the next five years, as far as the record shows, the byline Shakespeare was associated exclusively with those poems. Only after five years had passed was Shakespeare first named as a playwright. The identification came in Francis Meres's book *Palladis Tamia* (1598), which listed twelve plays by Shakespeare.[6] Only in that year did the name Shakespeare begin to appear on the printed plays. *Love's Labour's Lost* was the first. Until then, printed editions of the plays, six of them, had been anonymous. Again, a strange silence for a playwright, young and supposedly ambitious for success in the theater.

If Will Shakspere's early years raise questions, so do his final years. By Stratfordian chronology, no plays that are thought to be wholly Shakespeare's appeared after Will Shakspere was forty-eight years old. And he still had four more years to live, four years during which he was actively engaged in real estate transactions and Stratford affairs of highways and land enclosures. During those four years, he could have prepared the plays for publication, as Ben Jonson was doing at the same time for his own works. But he didn't. If he was the author, he not only ceased writing at the height of his creative powers, but appeared to take no interest in the work of his lifetime that had supposedly brought him fame and fortune.

Oxfordians maintain that Oxford's life span fits Shakespeare.[7] His seniority—he was fourteen years older than Will Shakspere—permits a more rational estimate of when the poems and plays were written. Oxford was in his late thirties, a mature man, when conventional chronology has the early plays of Shakespeare being written. If Oxford was Shakespeare, his creative production continued through his forties and up to his death at fifty-four. The last decade of his life was the decade that saw publication of nearly all the plays that first appeared in quarto editions, some anonymously, some as by Shakespeare. Oxfordians suggest that he had withdrawn from public life to concentrate on his poems and plays. They see him hard at work writing new plays, such as *The Tempest* and *King Lear*, rewriting old ones, and expanding some of them, notably *Hamlet*, for posterity. At Oxford's death, the printing of new plays ceased for nineteen years, with just four exceptions, until the *First Folio* was published with eighteen plays that had never before been printed.[8]

The timing of the first appearance of Shakespeare's name also fits Oxford's life span. Oxford was forty-three and forty-four years old when *Venus and Adonis* and *The Rape of Lucrece* were published with the dedications by Shakespeare. At about the same time Oxford seems to have withdrawn from his active life in the theater and literary circles. His name thereafter occurs infrequently in the records. J. Thomas Looney, the first Oxfordian, noted this provocative quirk of chronology, which suggests that at this time Oxford ceased to be known as a writer solely under his own name and became Shakespeare, whose poems and plays then began to appear in the records.

Whereas Stratfordians must struggle with evidence that seems to have Will Shakspere writing excellent plays very early in life, Oxfordians must look for early work by Oxford. Any early plays by him would be anonymous, because no plays under Oxford's name have been found. Some Oxfordians point to the titles and performance dates of eleven plays that appear in court records when Oxford was in his late twenties. He had returned from his travels on the Continent and was enjoying the queen's favor. No authors were named in the brief entries in the records. The texts have not survived. The plays, written for performance at court, may have been shorter, early versions of plays that were rewritten and expanded for performance in the public theaters. The expanded plays then appeared under new titles and under the Shakespeare byline.

This proposition is advanced by Eva Turner Clark in a book originally entitled *Shakespeare's Plays in the Order of Their Writing*.[9] She bases her proposition on similarity of titles between the eleven anonymous early plays and plays that later appeared as Shakespeare's. For example, one of the early titles was "The History of Error," which might have been an early version of *The Comedy of Errors*. Another handwritten title, "Titus and Gisippus," might have been an early *Titus Andronicus*, "Gisippus" being a name not found in Roman history and perhaps a mistranscription of "ronicus" in "And-ronicus." Clark notes the difficulty of accepting the mistranscription when rendered in modern printing, "but Elizabethan script is another matter." The title "The Rape of the Second Helen" might have been that of an early play renamed *All's Well That Ends Well*, the first Helen being Helen of Troy and the second Helen the heroine of *All's Well*, who tricks Bertram into sleeping with her in a sort of induced acquaintance rape. The eleven plays were registered between 1576, when Oxford was twenty-six (and Will Shakspere twelve), and 1580, when Oxford was thirty (and Will Shakspere sixteen).

Clark also finds hundreds of topical allusions in Shakespeare, which she correlates with historical events and personalities. The topical allusions seem to put the initial composition of the plays a decade earlier than in the conventional Stratfordian chronology. For example, she identifies allusions in the plays to the projected marriage of Queen Elizabeth and the French duke of Alençon, to troubles with Mary Queen of Scots and the Roman Catholics, and to the threat of invasion by the Spanish Armada. She argues that these allusions would have been old hat if they were in plays written for audiences a decade later, as Stratfordians believe. Clark's proposed chronology fits Oxford's life and times and seems to be a reasonable hypothesis in general.

Trying to fix the year of composition (and possibly revision) of Shakespeare's plays is risky business. Nevertheless, most Stratfordian scholars have felt obliged to put the plays into a conjectural chronological order. Their editions of the collected works force a sequencing of some sort. Despite their reservations about the evidence, their chronologies have, perhaps inevitably, taken on the aura of established fact. Oxfordian scholars, except for Clark, generally do not attempt to set years of composition of the plays and poems and put them all into chronological order. For them, too, the evidence is too uncertain.

Oxfordians see Shakespeare as a writer who continued to develop his skills as a dramatist and poetic artist over his lifetime. In this view, he was constantly revising, rewriting and improving his plays, sometimes adding references to political events to make them more timely. He began no later than his mid-twenties and early thirties with short plays or masques for performances at court. They see Oxford as Shakespeare reaching his maturity as a playwright in his late thirties and forties, when, in fact, the fully realized plays and poems attributed to Shakespeare began to appear. In his late forties and early fifties the plays poured from the presses, three in his forty-seventh year alone. Then, after his death at fifty-four only four new plays were published in quarto editions over the next two decades.

The Oxfordian view also describes a poet/dramatist who created from his own experience, as have all the great artists. The fiction of Count Leo Tolstoy is drawn from his life as a titled landowner, patriarch of an extended family, member of the ruling class, and officer in the army. The novels of Marcel Proust are based on his life, relatives, and friends in the Parisian haute bourgeoisie. The imaginative work of Miguel Cervantes paints a sweeping picture of life around him in Spain while debunking the romances of chivalry. Mark Twain's greatest works of fiction are drawn from his early life on the Mississippi River, Herman Melville's from his life on whaling ships. Kafka, Mann, Molière, Joyce, Dickens, Hemingway, Faulkner, O'Neill, Updike—all draw directly on what they have seen, heard, and learned, transmuting their experience into their most effective art.

The Stratfordian view requires that Will Shakspere be a radically different type of artist, his works far removed from the life he led. His life span presents problems. The first plays of Shakespeare appear before he is old enough to have gained the life experience required to write them. He stops writing at the peak of his creative years and retires to Stratford at least four years before his death. The main events of his life are not reflected in the works of Shakespeare. His youth as the glover's son in a small market town, his marriage to an older woman, his discovery of London and the theater, his real estate ventures—none of this is found in the works of Shakespeare in any significant way, if at all.

Through some miraculous power of genius Will Shakspere seemingly was able to write great literature while suppressing his own life experience and substituting the point of view and life experience of an aristocrat. Accepting the Stratfordian view has required a great leap of faith to embrace a type of genius that can somehow intuit experience.

No such leap of faith is required by the Oxfordian view of Shakespeare. Oxford's life not only fits Shakespeare, it is mirrored throughout the plays in so many particulars that it cannot be called mere coincidence. It is perhaps true that "literature and life are full of cunning parallels," as Schoenbaum believes.[10] One has to search long and hard, however, to find any direct parallels between the works of Shakespeare and the life of Will Shakspere of Stratford-on-Avon, whereas the parallels with the life of Oxford are many and striking, especially in *Hamlet*, usually considered the most autobiographical of Shakespeare's plays.

Chapter Ten

Oxford Revealed in Shakespeare's Plays

One day in May 1573 Lord Burghley received a letter complaining about an escapade of his twenty-three-year-old son-in-law, the seventeenth earl of Oxford. The letter was from two former servants of Oxford. They said they had been riding peaceably on the highway from Gravesend to Rochester when they were waylaid by three men who had lain hidden in a ditch. They identified the highwaymen as three of Oxford's men.

Shots were fired at close range, but no one was hit. The gunfire was so close, the letter said, that the saddle girth on one of the horses broke and the rider was thrown to the ground. The highwaymen then rode off toward London. "It pleased God to deliver us from that determined mischief," the victims told Burghley.

They went on to complain that the same men "beset our lodgings" in London and forced them to flee to Gravesend, where they still felt themselves to be in danger. They pleaded with Burghley to provide them with security from their attackers and from Oxford "as the procurer of that which is done."

Oxford may have been more than just the instigator. The victims mention his "raging demeanor," which suggests they saw him at the scene of the mischievous ambush. They do not accuse him of having been there, however, possibly out of deference to his rank or fear of offending him.[1]

The escapade is recounted in remarkably similar terms in Shakespeare's *Henry IV Part 1*. Prince Hal, who consorts with the lowlifes of the Boar's Head Tavern, goes along with Falstaff and three other rogues on a robbery caper at Gad's Hill, which is on the same road from Gravesend to Rochester. At one point Falstaff lies on the ground in ambush. After he and the band of rogues have robbed the travelers, Prince Hal and Poins, in disguise, compound the mischief by robbing the robbers and chasing them from the scene. All then return to London. Shakespeare gives the name Gadshill to one of the highwaymen.

The Gad's Hill escapade is only one of many specific allusions to incidents in Oxford's life that appear in the works of Shakespeare. The allusions are not just general allusions, such as any author might use in his writings. They are specific to events in Oxford's own life, and their accumulative weight is impressive.

The most notable allusions are to his experience as a ward of the crown, his marriage to his guardian's daughter, his affair with the queen's lady-in-waiting, his travels on the Continent, his patronage of writers and acting companies, and his concern for his reputation and good name.[2] The allusions occur in a number of plays, particularly *Hamlet*, which nearly everyone considers to be highly autobiographical, and in *All's Well That Ends Well*.[3] Both are often considered to be "problem plays," *Hamlet* being one of Shakespeare's best plays and *All's Well* one of his worst in the opinion of many critics.

ALL'S WELL THAT ENDS WELL

What bothers the critics about *All's Well* are the bitterness of the satire in a comedy, the disagreeable nature of the hero, and the forced, mechanical nature of the plot that ends unconvincingly.[4] Much becomes clear, however, for those who read the play with Oxford in mind as the author.

The plot line of *All's Well* seems to be drawn directly from Oxford's early life. His situation during his teenage years as a ward of the Crown and his marriage at twenty-one are closely paralleled by the play. As it opens, Bertram, the difficult young hero, has just become a ward of the crown upon the death of his father, a French count. A count in France is the equivalent of an earl in England. The heroine, Helena, daughter of the king's physician, induces the king to order Bertram to marry her over Bertram's objections that she is a commoner.

The parallels are manifold. Oxford, an earl and a ward of the Crown upon the death of his father, was betrothed to the daughter of William Cecil, Lord Burghley, the queen's chief councillor. Like the physician in the play, Burghley had also been born a commoner. In the play, the king promises to elevate Helena to a title. In real life the queen raised the Cecil family, including Anne, to nobility just before her wedding to Oxford.

In the play Bertram balks at the idea of marriage to Helena and says he'll run away to the wars. When the king forces him to marry Helena, he vows, "I will not bed her," and runs away to Italy. Oxford's marriage date was set and then postponed three months. A few years later, still childless, he ran away to the wars on the Continent, but was summoned home by the queen. He and his teenage bride were childless for more than three years, although ultimately they had five children, and for part of those three years, Oxford traveled in Italy.

The most remarkable correspondence, however, is the so-called bed trick, which is crucial to the plot of *All's Well* and which was reported to have actually happened to Oxford when he was twenty-four years old. In the bed trick, an unsuspecting husband, sometimes drunk, goes to bed in the dark with a woman he thinks is a prostitute or a new conquest, but who in reality is his virgin wife. The ploy, which derived from folklore, was supposed to trick an unwilling husband into consummating a marriage and perhaps producing an heir.

In the play an innkeeper's daughter agrees to lure the amorous Bertram into her bedroom late at night and thence into her bed. Helena takes her place in the bed and the unsuspecting Bertram is tricked in the dark into consummating the marriage. And all's well that ends well, more or less.

The same bed trick was reported to have happened to Oxford. A memoir left by a retainer of one of Oxford's sons-in-law mentions in passing "the last great Earl of Oxford, whose lady was brought to his bed under the notion of his mistress and from

such a virtuous deceit she [their daughter] is said to proceed."
The retainer who left the memoir worked for Philip Herbert, earl
of Montgomery, who was one of the two men to whom the *First
Folio* was dedicated. Even if the report is not true, which seems
possible, the fact that someone, and probably others, thought it
was true constitutes an amazing correspondence between Oxford's life and Shakespeare's play.[5]

Both the bed trick and royal wardship turn up in other plays
of Shakespeare. In *Measure for Measure*, Mariana pulls the bed
trick on an unwary Angelo, whom she wishes to seal in a con-
summated marriage. In *Cymbeline*, the hero again is a royal ward
who marries his guardian's daughter.

ROMEO AND JULIET

Scenes from Oxford's life also turn up in *Romeo and Juliet*. The
street fighting between the Montagues and the Capulets is
strongly reminiscent of the street fighting between Oxford's men
and Thomas Knyvet's men. The play opens with a clash in the
streets of Verona between Romeo and his family, the Montagues,
and Juliet's family, the Capulets. In real life, Oxford and his men
clashed with Knyvet and his men in London, and Oxford received a serious wound. Knyvet was part of a rival political fac-
tion and also a cousin of Anne Vavasor, Oxford's lover and
mother of his illegitimate son. Both in the play and in real life,
men are killed in street fighting, and a higher authority inter-
venes to try to stop the brawling. In the play it is Prince Escalus
of Verona; in London it was Queen Elizabeth's councillors. The
family feud involving Romeo and Juliet mirrors the feud between rival factions involving Oxford and Anne Vavasor.[6]

THE MERCHANT OF VENICE

A provocative "coincidence" involving loans and investments
occurs in *The Merchant of Venice*.[7] In the play Antonio, a Venetian
merchant, posts bond with Shylock, the moneylender, as security
for three thousand ducats borrowed by a friend. Antonio's bond
is secured by a pound of flesh that Shylock may cut from his
body, but Antonio is not worried. He expects the return of three

merchant ships with rich cargoes in time to pay Shylock the three thousand ducats and be released from the bond. But the ships are lost at sea, and Shylock demands his pound of flesh.

Oxford pledged his bond for the same amount in pounds—three thousand—to invest in the third of three Frobisher voyages seeking a northwest passage to the riches of Asia or, failing that, gold ore. Most of his investment was in shares sold by Michael Lok, a London merchant. The ships returned with no treasure, and the enterprise went bankrupt. Lok was accused of swindling the investors, who besieged his house, and was imprisoned.

Lok's name was sometimes spelled Lock. With the prefix "shy," which can mean disreputable or shady, Michael Lock, the merchant of London, becomes Shylock, the moneylender in *The Merchant of Venice*. The name Shylock is unique; scholars have not been able to find any precedents for it.[8] Shakespeare seems to have made it up, lending credence to the "shy"- Lok theory. Oxfordians also find in the play a number of derogatory allusions to Burghley, who effectively controlled Oxford's finances and forced him to sell properties to pay wardship debts.

HAMLET

But of all the plays, *Hamlet* produces the greatest number of parallels to Oxford's life. For many it clinches the case for Oxford as the author Shakespeare. Even those who have never considered that Oxford might be the author sense that of all the plays *Hamlet* is the one that most closely reflects the author's life and personal concerns. The hero could not have been created by a writer who was very different from Hamlet.[9]

The play is Shakespeare's longest by far. Uncut, it runs four to five hours, suggesting that the author went beyond simply writing a revenge play for the theatergoers at the Globe. The play seems to be a profound reflection on the author's life and concerns. It is pervaded by the pressure of personal emotion.

From Hamlet's first appearance in the play to his dying words, echoes of Oxford's life are everywhere. In the second scene Hamlet deplores his widowed mother's remarriage, with "most wicked speed," to a man much inferior to his father. Oxford's mother remarried after her husband's death while Oxford was still in his teens. (The marriage date has not been found.) Her second husband was Charles Tyrell, a commoner of no special distinction who was far beneath her rank as the countess of Oxford. When she died, she was buried with her first husband, the sixteenth earl. When Charles Tyrell died, his bequest to Oxford was a horse that Oxford had given him.[10]

No records survive about Oxford's relations with his mother except for one letter she wrote to Burghley, her son's guardian, regarding her husband's estate. She mentions her son, then thirteen, only in passing. Beyond that, the record is silent. In the plays of Shakespeare mothers who show warm maternal feelings toward their children are notable by their absence.

With the characters of Ophelia and Polonius the play *Hamlet* comes closest to the life of Oxford. Ophelia is the young daughter of Polonius, councillor to the king. She is supposed to marry Hamlet. Anne Cecil was the daughter of Burghley, chief minister to the queen. Before she was fifteen she was betrothed to Oxford, and she ultimately was married to him, although the marriage was postponed once. Ophelia on stage and Anne Cecil in real life were both young girls under the sway of powerful rulers and councillors in the royal court. Both were daughters of commoners and both were destined by their elders for marriage to young aristocrats of noble blood.

Polonius has long been considered a caricature of Burghley, Oxford's guardian and then father-in-law.[11] Shakespearean scholars in the nineteenth century recognized the caricature decades before anyone thought Oxford might be the author. Since then, even scholars who ignore or dismiss the possibility that Oxford was Shakespeare have generally accepted the identification of Polonius as Burghley. The evidence is quite convincing.

The author of *Hamlet*, whoever he was, probably not only knew Burghley, but was closely associated with him. The principal evidence for this close association is Polonius's advice to his son, Laertes, in the string of maxims that ends, "This above all, to thy own self be true." Polonius's maxims are a parody of Burghley's long-winded advice in a letter to his own son. Burghley's letter, however, was not printed until years after he, Oxford, and Will Shakspere were dead. To produce the parody, the author of *Hamlet* must have seen Burghley's precepts in an early manuscript form or heard about them. Oxford would have been perfectly placed not only to see or hear about Burghley's precepts, but to have been inspired to parody them. (There are no records that Will Shakspere of Stratford ever met Burghley or had anything to do with him.)

Polonius was Burghley in name as well as in character. The name's probable origin shows that it was not picked at random but had insider connotations for those in the queen's court. Two contemporary notes have been found that refer to Burghley by the nicknames "Polus" and "Pondus," both easily combined and transmuted into the Polonius of the play.

Furthermore, the character Polonius had a different name in an early version of the play, a name that could also be linked to Burghley, but more disparagingly. In the first quarto version the character's name is Corambis. Burghley's Latin motto was "Cor unum, via una," that is, "one heart, one way." By substituting "ambis" for "unum" after "Cor," the author created a name of doubleness instead of singularity. "Bis" means twice or again. It could be heard as signifying double-hearted, suggesting double-dealing or devious. The name Corambis, with its pejorative connotation, was changed to Polonius in later editions of the play. Only an author who was an insider at court would be likely to create this sequence of nicknames based on Burghley's character and reputation.

References to Lord Burghley abound in *Hamlet*. Burghley was well known for his spying tactics, even to the point of having spies report on his own son while the son was in Paris. Polonius has spies report on his son while the son is in Paris.

Hamlet kills Polonius while the councillor is spying on him from behind a curtain, but makes light of the slaying, almost as if it were symbolic, not real. He later tells the king mockingly that "a certain convocation of worms" is working on Polonius, adding that "your worm is your only emperor for diet." Burghley expressed pride in having been born during the Diet of Worms, a convocation of church and secular leaders in the German city named Worms and presided over by the emperor.

Hamlet calls Polonius a "fishmonger"; Burghley sponsored a law that made Wednesday a meatless day, in addition to Friday, in order to support the fishing industry and fishmongers.

The set of allusions to Burghley, first minister to the queen and Oxford's guardian and then father-in-law, are multiple, pointed, and specific. Stratfordian scholars recognize them, but do not explain how Will Shakspere of Stratford could have conceived them or, if he did, how he could have escaped public censure and punishment for ridiculing Lord Burghley, even after Burghley's death. (One of Burghley's sons succeeded him.) Oxfordians conclude that the allusions point inevitably to the seventeenth earl of Oxford as the author, the insider at court whose rank in the nobility and favored status with the queen and then with King James protected him from reprisals.

The allusions in *Hamlet* to Oxford's life are sometimes direct and extended, sometimes short and subtle, merely throwaway lines. At one point in act 2, Hamlet says, for no particular reason, "I am but mad north-north-west." The line makes little sense in the play, unless it's an allusion to the investment that Oxford lost in the expedition that was seeking a northwest passage to Asia. If Oxford was the author, he was making a jibe at his own expense.

Hamlet reports that his ship was set upon by pirates while he was on his way to England; Oxford's ship was twice set upon by pirates while he was returning to England.

Hamlet appears at one point reading an unidentified book. Some Stratfordian scholars like to suggest that the book must be *Cardanus Comforte* because so much of the book's philosophy is reflected in the play. Several scholarly articles have been written on the book's role in *Hamlet*. The first of them was published in the nineteenth century, long before Oxford was proposed as the author Shakespeare.[12]

Oxford knew the book well. He commissioned it and wrote a long preface addressed to the man who translated it from the Italian. The importance of Oxford's role in the book's publication is shown by the fact that Oxford's name, but not that of the translator, appears on the title page.

Hamlet commands, organizes, and stages the play within the play as an author, producer, and director—not as an actor. He is an enthusiastic, well-known patron of the visiting troupe of actors. They readily take his direction in authorial and technical aspects of the performances that he adapts in order to "catch the conscience of the king." Oxford was an active patron of acting companies, and he wrote and produced plays and was in a position to help direct them. Oxfordians maintain that one of his purposes in some of the plays was to catch the conscience of the queen.

Hamlet's most trusted friend is Horatio. One of Oxford's favorite cousins was Horatio de Vere, fifteen years his junior. Horatio took charge of Oxford's son Henry during a military campaign on the Continent. At one point, when Oxford was in his twenties, he reportedly wanted to make Horatio and Horatio's brother the heirs to his earldom.[13]

Hamlet's dying words to Horatio strike a note of powerful poignancy for those who become convinced that Oxford as Shakespeare revealed himself most intimately in *Hamlet*. The dying Hamlet for some reason implores Horatio to tell the true story about the events depicted in the play.[14] If Hamlet's words are also taken to represent Oxford's anguished cry that posterity may never link his name with the work of his lifetime, printed under the pen name William Shakespeare, then the passages carry a devastating message: "Horatio," says Hamlet, "I am dead. Thou livest. Report me and my cause aright to the unsatisfied."

Horatio tries to join Hamlet in death by drinking the poison that killed the queen, but Hamlet stops him and says:

> O God, Horatio, what a wounded name,
> Things standing thus unknown, shall live behind me.
> If thou didst ever hold me in thy heart,
> Absent thee from felicity a while,
> And in this harsh world draw thy breath in pain
> To tell my story.

Chapter Eleven

Objections to Oxford as Shakespeare

"They think that only an earl or a duke could really write plays like that, when you and I know what rot that is."

The speaker is Professor A. L. Rowse, a British historian and staunch defender of the Stratfordian faith. Aging but alert, feisty, and self-assured, he's being interviewed on a PBS-TV "Frontline" program about Oxford as the possible author. The setting is "the Birthplace" at Stratford-on-Avon.[1]

Rowse continues: "It's always the clever grammar school boys who write the plays, you know, like Christopher Marlowe or Ben Jonson or Nashe or Robert Greene or any of them. The plays are never written by an earl."

The objection is a familiar one. Substituting an aristocratic courtier to the queen for the Stratford glover's son as the author Shakespeare seems much too radical. That two such different men could both be proposed as the poet/dramatist is hard to believe. After all the years of research and scholarship, certainly the incumbent must be the true author. Besides, earls don't write plays.

Oxfordians, of course, see no reason why genius should be found only in commoners. They cite Count Tolstoy, Lord Byron, and other aristocrats who became artists of the first rank. The Stratfordian objection, they say, is inspired by a proletarian belief that anyone could have written the works of Shakespeare regardless of background and experience.[2] "Genius" would explain everything and carry all before it.

The most forceful objection to Oxford, especially for the general reader, is probably the "implausible conspiracy" objection.[3] Stratfordians argue that a widespread and long-lasting conspiracy would have been required to conceal Oxford's authorship and set up Will Shakspere as the decoy author. Such a conspiracy they find totally implausible. They also raise three other major objections: Francis Meres named both Shakespeare and Oxford as contemporary playwrights, thus they must have been two different men. A dozen plays made their first appearance years after Oxford died, thus he couldn't have been the author. Finally, another implausibility, Shakespeare's dedications to the third earl of Southhampton do not sound at all like what the seventeenth earl of Oxford, the lord great chamberlain, a man in his forties, would write to a young nobleman in his teens.

If Oxford was the author, so goes the implausible conspiracy argument, the secret could not have been kept. It would have leaked. Some record of it would have been found. Oxford was the ranking nobleman in the court, a favorite of the queen, a published author, and patron of acting companies. Anyone who knew anything about the court, the theater, and the milieu of writers and printers had to know whether he was the writer of the poems and plays that appeared as by Shakespeare. In fact, his authorship would have been notorious, even scandalous, since "plays are never written by an earl."

Still, there is no record by anyone during Oxford's lifetime or in the decades that followed that openly names him as the author behind the pseudonym Shakespeare. At no time did he himself openly claim authorship. No manuscripts, drafts, or notes have been found. Nothing from his son or illegitimate son about his authorship. Nothing, either, from his three surviving daughters, even though they lived on for decades after his death and were active in court and literary circles. Two of the daughters were married to earls who were closely involved with publication of the *First Folio*, which links Shakespeare's plays to the "sweet swan of Avon." His authorship was accepted for more than two hundred years, until well into the nineteenth century, when the first serious challenges appeared. It is inconceivable that centuries of scholarship should be overturned at this late date. Oxford's authorship could only have been concealed by an extensive and most implausible conspiracy involving a whole culture and lasting an indefinite amount of time. Stratfordians cannot accept such an implausible conspiracy.

Oxfordians respond that no such conspiracy was required. Oxford's authorship was simply an open secret, one that could not be publicly acknowledged. They find in the plays bold and incisive commentary on court affairs and even dangerous satire that would have required punishment if the commentary and the author's name had not been disguised. Stern action to suppress or condemn would have been expected. Apparently, no one in power wanted that to happen to the author. As long as the criticism and satire were veiled in good Elizabethan fashion, the Crown could turn a blind eye to the topical commentary, critiques, and satire. No one in authority would be forced to do something about it.

Only someone enjoying the queen's protection could have gotten away with the satire and commentary on court affairs. Oxford was in a position to enjoy such protection. He was the ranking earl of the realm, a favorite courtier of the queen, and the son-in-law of Lord Burghley, her closest adviser. It appears to have been a stand-off in a political power struggle. Oxford would be allowed to deliver his commentary on court affairs, perhaps even for the amusement of the sportive queen, but not under his own name and title.

If Oxford was the author Shakespeare, the fact of it would have been known to those in the know, but their number was probably quite small. By modern standards, London was a small city of less than 200,000 people, smaller than White Plains, New York, or New London/Norwich, Connecticut, which happens also to be located on a river called the Thames. Most Londoners of the time were illiterate. The literacy rate in Elizabethan London is estimated to have been fifteen to thirty percent.[4] A very rough guess at the number of people, ranging from queen to actors to typesetters, who would know that Oxford was the author and Will Shakspere the decoy might be in the low hundreds. Nearly all of them probably had a stake in complying with the wishes, spoken or unspoken, of the autocratic government, that is, Queen Elizabeth and Lord Burghley. Only a few were in a position to leave any revealing records that would be saved for posterity. It is doubtful that many theatergoers knew who wrote the plays, or that they cared. Authors were not the celebrities they are today. In short, there was no need for a mass literary conspiracy; it was Elizabethan business as usual. Oxford's authorship was an open secret.

Open secrets in state affairs are not unusual. Even with the intense scrutiny of the media on government and public affairs in modern times, those in power have been able to conceal what was an open secret for those near the inner circles of power. Most American voters were generally unaware of the facts about President Kennedy's womanizing, President Roosevelt's crippling polio, and President Wilson's disabling stroke. The power structure, including the media, was able to downplay and largely conceal inconvenient facts that might damage their leader's position in power. It was self-censorship. How much easier such concealment would have been in Elizabethan times, when there was no independent press that had responsibilities to an electorate and no hesitation by the Crown to exercise its powers of censorship.[5]

Censorship in Elizabethan times, by all accounts, was enforced by brutal methods. Torture, mutilation, branding, or imprisonment were routinely inflicted on those whose writings displeased the Crown. John Stubbs had his hand lopped off for writing that the queen might be better off not marrying a Frenchman. Ben Jonson, who later became, in effect, the queen's poet laureate, was imprisoned twice for his writings. He narrowly escaped execution once and was branded on the thumb. Writing about current events was a risky business. Arrest and punishment were ever-present threats, and could be arbitrary.

If anyone did write something identifying Oxford as Shakespeare, Burghley, acting in his and the queen's interest, could easily have had it expunged from the public record. Again, no conspiracy would be required. Burghley and his government were the record-keepers, and no one in the ruling class would have any reason to disobey or expose the censorship. Oxfordians like to hope that Burghley may have missed some records that will be discovered when researchers put as much time and effort into Oxford's life as they have into Will Shakspere's.

If Queen Elizabeth's successor, King James I, and his minister, Robert Cecil, who was Lord Burghley's son, wanted to enforce the use of the pseudonym, they had the same full powers of censorship. If they wanted to lend credence to Will Shakspere as the decoy author, they had only to order it done. No one knows who ordered the ambiguous inscription affixed to the Stratford monument. However it was done, no conspiracy was required. England was ruled by an autocracy that by and large could do as it thought most expedient to maintain its public position. At some point, probably late in Oxford's life or even after his death, Will Shakspere, once a theater personage and more lately a wealthy landowner of Stratford-on-Avon, was to be considered the author, if anyone asked.

An important aspect of the "implausible conspiracy" objection is motivation: why Oxford and the court and his family should go to the trouble of suppressing public recognition of his authorship, especially after his death. Oxford, Queen Elizabeth, and Lord Burghley had all been dead for two decades when the *First Folio* was published in 1623. There is no apparent reason why Oxford's authorship of the plays, if he was the author, could not have been recognized with publication of the *First Folio*. With all three principals dead for twenty years, the continued nature of the conspiracy to hide Oxford's authorship appears highly implausible to Stratfordians.

Oxfordians respond that Elizabethan records show that it was generally considered disgraceful for a nobleman to write plays for the public theater or publish anything under his own name. With few exceptions, none did so during their lifetimes. Oxford's heirs may well have felt the same way, while at the same time wanting to preserve the plays and poems for posterity. They may have continued to use the pseudonym Shakespeare because that was the name on the already published poems and plays; there was no reason not to continue using it. There was no secret to be disclosed at last. Those who cared knew the identity of the man behind the pseudonym, why he used it, and why no one could publicly acknowledge his use of it. They knew the open secret.[6]

An additional difficulty for Stratfordians is the use of Will Shakspere as the decoy author. They find it totally implausible that anyone would accept such a deception if Will Shakspere was, in fact, not the author of the poems and plays. Anyone involved in literature and the theater would know he was not the author, especially if he was the uneducated, semiliterate, Stratford-based, bit-part actor that Oxfordians make him out to be. No one interested in poetry and plays could have been deceived.

If Will Shakspere was a decoy, the monument in the Stratford church becomes a superfluous ruse erected by authorities who had better things to worry about. Honest Ben Jonson becomes a liar with his testimony about the River Avon in the *First Folio*. Will Shakspere's onetime neighbor, Leonard Digges, becomes a liar with his words about "thy Stratford moniment." The two actor friends, Heminge and Condell, are guilty of testifying falsely about their knowledge of the authorship and how they got the manuscripts of the plays together for publication. A totally implausible concatenation of events, according to Stratfordians.

Oxfordians take this all in stride and offer an explanation. Will Shakspere's imputed authorship was a sham, a smokescreen behind which the queen and Lord Burghley could escape any need to take action to curb Oxford, a leading nobleman of the realm and a favorite courtier of the queen herself, or to suppress his allegorical commentaries, which the queen may have found most entertaining and even enlightening. After all, she did authorize payment of an enormous lifetime annuity to Oxford, possibly for his theatrical productions. Ben Jonson and Leonard Digges were not liars; they practiced careful ambiguity in the *First Folio*. Heminge and Condell, two lowly actors, did what they were told. It's possible they never even reviewed the dedicatory letters written by Ben Jonson to which their names were affixed.

No one suggests that Will Shakspere spent most of his life in London as the decoy author. After all, he himself never claimed authorship, whether real or decoy. When the name Shakespeare first began to appear on the plays, the records show that Will

Shakspere began to have more business and legal affairs in Strat-ford-on-Avon than in London. Within ten years or so he is sup-posed to have stopped writing and retired to his hometown. Only seven years after he died was there any testimony linking him to the plays of Shakespeare, namely in the *First Folio*.

Stratfordians might also print out that the foisting of a pseu-donym onto a real person is unique in literature for an author of any importance. If Oxford wrote Shakespeare, the application of his pseudonym to a real person who was not the author (i.e., Will Shakspere of Stratford) is unprecedented and thus hard to accept. Oxfordians agree that it is unique, but argue that it is the only reasonable interpretation of the evidence. They do not as-sert that Oxford himself was behind it; they can only offer con-jecture on how it came about and how the pseudonym happened to be so similar to the name of the man from Stratford.[7]

If accepting Oxford's authorship means accepting a decoy au-thor in an implausible conspiracy, as Stratfordians would have it, belief in Will Shakspere of Stratford-on-Avon as the author requires an even more unlikely conspiracy—a conspiracy of si-lence. Any direct references to the Stratford man personally dur-ing his lifetime as the famous poet and playwright of London must have disappeared. Records showing that he could write anything at all and any proofs of literary associations or en-deavors must have been suppressed. He himself, or someone, must have persuaded those who knew him not to leave any re-cords about him personally as a writer of poems and plays, even at his death. The printers had to be told to spell his name Shake-speare, although in Stratford-on-Avon and in his business life the Stratford spelling was the customary spelling. From this point of view, if Will Shakspere really was the author, it is *his* life story that must be the result of an "implausible conspiracy."

Besides the objection of implausible conspiracy, Stratfordian scholars often cite Oxford's life span, and in particular his death in 1604, as a major difficulty to his being the poet/dramatist Shakespeare. Schoenbaum calls it "the principal drawback of the entire argument."[8] He notes that ten of the plays appeared on the stage after Oxford was buried, but he carries the argument no further. The *Encyclopedia Britannica*, which calls Oxford "the strongest candidate" for the authorship of the plays outside of

Will Shakspere, also cites Oxford's death date as a major difficulty. Explaining the difficulty, the article states that fourteen of the plays were "first staged" after Oxford's death.[9]

The issue, however, is when the plays were written, not when they were first staged. Posthumous production would not be unusual for any playwright. Moreover, the argument, if it were valid, would also deny Will Shakspere's authorship. Three of the plays were not staged or even mentioned in records until after Will Shakspere had died, too, thereby presenting the identical major difficulty to his authorship. The objection, of course, is specious whether applied to Oxford or Will Shakspere; premieres can and do occur after a playwright's death.

The Tempest is often cited as late play that Oxford could not have written because it seems to refer to a shipwreck that occurred after his death. The first recorded mention of the play was in 1611, seven years after Oxford died. The source for the shipwreck reference is said to have been the 1610 report of a shipwreck in Bermuda, six years after Oxford died. In the play, Ariel recalls that Prospero once sent him "to fetch dew from the still-vexed Bermoothes." Bermoothes is a variant spelling for the Bermudas, the Atlantic Ocean islands. "Still-vexed" is supposed to mean continually afflicted by tempests.

Oxfordians reject both the interpretation of Ariel's line and the continued use of the 1610 Bermuda shipwreck report to date the play. The 1610 report proves nothing. Shipwrecks had been reported in the Bermudas decades earlier, well before Oxford's death. In fact, a ship that Oxford owned was involved in a shipwreck in the Bermudas during his lifetime. There was no need for the author of *The Tempest* to read a 1610 report to know about shipwrecks in the Bermuda islands.

Furthermore, Ariel may not have been referring to the "Bermoothes" as the islands in the Atlantic Ocean at all. Prospero's enchanted island of the play is located in the Mediterranean Sea, not the Atlantic. And the storm-battered ship was not wrecked; it was "safely in harbor," according to Ariel. Richard Roe, an Oxfordian scholar, has pointed out that "Bermoothes," or Bermudas, was also the name of a section of London known as the haunt of loafers, toughs, and heavy drinkers. In sending Ariel "to fetch dew from the still-vexed Bermoothes," Prospero might have been sending Ariel to a bar and distillery in the Bermoothes section of London to fetch some of its "dew."[10] A local joke.

Two major objections to Oxford's authorship are based on a passage in *Palladis Tamia,* a book by an obscure clergyman named Francis Meres.[11] It was published in 1598, six years before Oxford died and the year that Will Shakspere turned thirty-four. The six-hundred-page book is almost entirely a collection of miscellaneous anecdotes, similes and sayings, grouped in moral and religious sections. The book contains nothing of significance except for sixteen pages in the middle of it. In these pages, Meres gives literary assessments of no less than 125 English writers and artists, comparing them all favorably to classical and Italian Renaissance writers and artists. He lauds Shakespeare as "most excellent" for comedy and tragedy and names twelve plays by him. Oxford heads a list of seventeen writers whom Meres calls "best for comedy," a list that also includes Shakespeare. He gives no biographical information about any of the writers.

The first objection based on Meres's book is simply stated: Meres named Oxford first among the playwrights who were "best for comedy" in a listing that also included Shakespeare. He wrote about Oxford and Shakespeare as two different men, each deserving mention by name. Therefore, the two were known as separate individuals, and Oxford could not have been Shakespeare.

Oxfordians contend there is no problem: Meres was simply reflecting the fact that Oxford was known as a writer of plays for the court and the private theater anonymously, and also as a writer of published poetry and plays either anonymously or under his pseudonym Shakespeare. Meres could not omit either name without appearing ignorant about the theater and the reputations of contemporary playwrights. Nor could he publicly acknowledge the open secret that Oxford wrote Shakespeare's plays. He could, however, list both names, knowing that his readers would understand his meaning, if any even paid attention when they reached the middle of his thick book of anecdotes, similes, and quotations. Meres's book was not about the London theater. In its day, it was just another commonplace book of sayings and quotations.

The second objection to Oxford that is based on Meres's book is more complex. It involves fitting the plays into Oxford's life span. Stratfordians note that Meres named only twelve plays, leaving twenty-four to be accounted for by Oxfordians, whose man died just six years later. (Will Shakspere had eighteen more years to live.) And Meres did not include *Hamlet, Lear, Henry V, The Winter's Tale*, and other plays that Oxfordians say were written before Meres published his book. Stratfordians find it inconceivable that Meres would omit such plays from his list if indeed they had been written and performed.

In a 1991 *Atlantic Monthly* issue on Shakespeare and Oxford, the Stratfordian Irvin Matus maintains that Oxford would have had to write eighteen or more plays in the last six years of his life, an impossibility. Matus arrives at eighteen by taking Meres's twelve plays and adding the five or six more that scholars generally agree were written before Meres published but were not named by him. That accounts for about half of the thirty-six plays in the *First Folio*. So the other eighteen had to be written in the six years between the publication of Meres's book and Oxford's death. For Matus and other Stratfordians the arithmetic precludes Oxford as the author. In his book (1994), Matus accepts twenty-five plays as having been written by the time Meres's book was published, with eleven or twelve still to be written in the next six years, if they are by Oxford. The numbers change, but the point of his argument remains.[12]

Oxfordians reply that Meres's list was obviously incomplete even by Stratfordian standards. Therefore, many more plays could have been written before Meres published, including *Hamlet, Lear*, and others that Stratfordians date after Meres's book. That Meres would omit several major plays is perhaps puzzling, but Meres was a minister, not a literary or theater critic. It is worth repeating that no firm evidence exists for the composition dates of the poems and plays, including those that first appeared after Oxford's death.

Oxfordians note that Meres's comments on London writers were totally out of character for him, based on his other writings. He was a Protestant minister who translated religious works. In the same year as *Palladis Tamia*, he published translations of three religious works written by a Spanish mystic. He never published anything else to the end of his life, nearly half a century later.

Most of his life was spent in a rectory in northern England. Never again did he appear in the records of the London literary scene.

The sixteen pages in the middle of his book are a striking contrast with his life. He lists 125 English writers and artists, and his comments about them are pithy and perspicacious, suggesting great familiarity. For example, Anthony Munday is "our best plotter," George Peele died "by the pox," Drayton "is termed golden-mouthed for the purity and pretiousness of his style and phrase," Shakespeare circulated his "sugered sonnets among his private friends." There is, however, no corroborative evidence that he ever frequented literary circles in London. Inevitably, questions about Meres's role and credibility have been raised by Oxfordians.

Those who object to Oxford as the author sometimes cite the difficulty of accepting as his the dedications in *Venus and Adonis* and *The Rape of Lucrece*, the two narrative poems. They describe the tone of the two dedications as fawning, even groveling to modern ears, and totally inappropriate from the ranking earl of England, who was twice Southampton's age. Instead, say the Stratfordians, the dedications by Will Shakspere the commoner confirm that he had gained a close, personal friend in the nobility.

Oxfordians reject the image of the dedications as fawning or groveling. They describe them as dignified, self-assured, even intimate, especially when compared to the florid declamations typical of the time. Some Oxfordians see the dedications as evidence, yet to be validated, that there was a highly unusual relationship between Oxford and Southampton, the former old enough to be the father of the latter. Whatever the relationship, Oxford at least knew Southampton. The young man was a ward of Burghley, Oxford's father-in-law. A few years earlier, Oxford's daughter had been proposed by Burghley, her grandfather, as a husband for Southampton. Southampton refused and paid a heavy fine.

No evidence exists that Will Shakspere ever knew Southampton. Oxfordians find it impossible to believe that Will Shakspere, the twenty-nine-year-old theater personage from Stratford, wrote the dedications to Southampton, a hereditary lord and at the time a ward in Burghley's household. Class distinctions were rigid. The language seems much too self-assured, even bold and presumptuous, for a commoner addressing a nobleman. Furthermore, there is no record of any other link between them, neither earlier nor later. It's difficult to understand why the glover's son from Stratford would fail to follow up if he had the extraordinary patronage of a nobleman.

Other objections to Oxford as the author that occur less frequently include the following:[13]

1. There are so many candidates for authorship that none can be valid; the claims cancel out each other. Oxfordians argue the reverse: the intense search confirms the validity of the widespread doubt about Will Shakspere and the need to fill the void; and just because fifty-nine candidates are not credible does not mean number sixty should be dismissed, too.

2. It is wrong and self-serving for Oxfordians to argue that all the contemporary literary allusions and references to Shakespeare are to the poet/dramatist, "whoever he was," and then to deny that they refer to Will Shakspere of Stratford-on-Avon. Oxfordians make two points. First, the literary allusions and references do not identify Shakespeare as an actual, living, identifiable person; they refer only to Shakespeare the poet/dramatist, whoever he was. Second, the main point of all the challenges to Will Shakspere as the author is that the name Shakespeare was not his, but was a pseudonym. To make the all-too-easy assumption that the name Shakespeare equals the man Will Shakspere wherever the name appears is to ignore the difference between the two and beg the question.

3. Sonnet 136 concludes with the words "for my name is Will," certainly indicating that Will Shakspere wrote it. (Few raise this point.) Oxfordians note that it would be puerile for Shakespeare to refer to himself that way. Sonnets 135 and 136 are extended bawdy wordplays on various meanings of "will." The word occurs twenty times in twenty-eight lines.

Fundamental for those who reject Oxford as Shakespeare is the conviction that the thousands of scholars who have studied the life and works of Shakespeare over three centuries can't all be wrong. The idea is, indeed, daunting. Nothing like the continuing doubt about Shakespeare's identity has occurred in literature. No precedent exists.

Precedents do exist, however, in science. Long-held beliefs, supported by academic scholarship, have been overturned, but only after decades and even centuries of struggle and sometimes acrimonious wrangling. Among them are the Galilean and Darwinian revolutions and the recent acceptance by establishment geologists of plate tectonics, proposed, as it happens, by an amateur geologist.

To give up Will Shakspere of Stratford-on-Avon as the author would not be easily done. Millions of tourists have paid homage to him at "the Birthplace" in Stratford-on-Avon. Hundreds of millions have accepted the laconic descriptions of the Stratford man in English literature textbooks, in introductions to editions of the plays and poems, and in notes about the author in theater programs. New biographies of Will Shakspere of Stratford-on-Avon, or books including his standard biography, appear every year. Thousands of Shakespearean scholars have inherited the Stratfordian belief, expounded in thousands of books and articles for almost two centuries. Quite understandably, they may be reluctant to question and perhaps jettison their hard-won knowledge, expertise, and reputation.

Oxfordians acknowledge the difficulty Stratfordians would encounter if they were to consider the possibility that Oxford was the true author. But they cite the novelist Henry James, who wrote to a friend, "I am 'a sort of' haunted by the conviction that the divine William is the biggest and most successful fraud ever practiced on a patient world."[14]

And they cite Shakespeare: "For truth is truth to the end of reckoning."

And they cite the words of Edward de Vere, seventeenth earl of Oxford: "For truth is truth, though never so old, and time cannot make that false which once was true."

Chapter Twelve

Resolving the Authorship Issue

Maybe it's all coincidence.

Maybe Oxford's life just happens to fit perfectly the profile of Shakespeare that would be drawn by someone who had read the works of Shakespeare but who, one might imagine, had never heard of Will Shakspere of Stratford-on-Avon. Maybe some other lord would fit just as well, if he could be found.

Maybe all the parallels in Shakespeare's works to specific events and relationships in Oxford's life are simply happenstance. Maybe Polonius is not Burghley, and *Hamlet* only seems to be autobiographical.

Maybe Will Shakspere took an incredibly keen interest in the private and public lives of Oxford and Burghley in some way that no one has discovered.

Maybe it's coincidental that Oxford's sons-in-law were closely involved with Ben Jonson in publishing the *First Folio* of Shakespeare's plays. Maybe the ambiguities in the prefatory letters and verses to the *First Folio* are just poetic license, innocent of any significance.

Maybe the plays of Oxford under his own name (not being those of Shakespeare) were simply lost or discarded by the acting companies and never printed, even though he was extolled as an excellent playwright.

Maybe Will Shakspere read and heard about the manners and mores of nobility and royalty—from the game of bowls to power politics—that fill Shakespeare's works. Maybe his activities and passions happened to coincide with Oxford's—from wardship under Burghley to military command, court intrigues, law and courtroom trials, the culture of France and Italy, and even to specific books, such as Ovid's *Metamorphoses* and *Cardanus Comforte*.

Maybe Will Shakspere was in fact an ambitious, hard-working actor, poet, and dramatist of superhuman genius who nevertheless shunned any personal recognition and persuaded his contemporaries to keep quiet. And spell his name Shakespeare.

Maybe the total silence at his death and for seven years afterwards was for some unknown reason a conspiracy of silence. Maybe the engraved portrait and Stratford monument were just the result of ignorant and sloppy workmanship.

On and on, the "maybes" multiply beyond belief. A few would be understandable when dealing with events four centuries ago. So many "maybes" are what have led to the continuing doubts about the case for Will Shakspere as the poet/dramatist and to the growing support for Edward de Vere, seventeenth earl of Oxford, as the true author.

The parallels between the life of Oxford and the works of Shakespeare are too numerous and too striking to be dismissed as coincidence or insignificant. Their cumulative effect is impressive and calls for an explanation. In a court of law enough parallels or "coincidences," which are called evidence, will lead a jury to convict a defendant, even without the defendant's admission or an irrefutable eyewitness. The cumulative weight of the evidence leads to a verdict.

This book has tried to present the evidence for both sides in an evenhanded way, although the case for Oxford does seem most persuasive. If it were not, there would be no reason even to put the Shakespeare authorship question to a jury of general readers for their consideration. To expect, however, that many will be persuaded by this summary of the evidence for Oxford so that they will switch their allegiance would be presumptuous. The objective is more modest: to persuade the general reader that the controversy is valid and genuinely fascinating, that Oxford may indeed be the true author, and that more research should be done into this most significant of literary problems.

For many, the greatest hurdle to considering Oxford as the author is the difficulty of accepting the possibility that for centuries the wrong man has been taken to be the author of the works of Shakespeare. Will Shakspere continues to enjoy the support of the establishment authorities in academia and publishing. They have inherited a powerful tradition. The image of the glove maker's son from Stratford-on-Avon has become part of our cultural heritage. He is an icon of Western civilization, for some still an idol to be worshipped as the immortal Bard of Avon who came from humble beginnings.

Anyone who questions the traditional and quasi-religious belief in the Bard and who would propose someone else as the author bears, perhaps unfairly, the burden of proof. In the introduction to his book, R. C. Churchill, an ardent Stratfordian, asserts in no uncertain terms: "That William Shakespeare of Stratford wrote the plays and poems commonly attributed to him is not a *theory* at the present time, it is a *fact* at the present time—and will continue to be a fact until it is definitely proved wrong." (Emphases in original.) Oxfordians chafe at having to bear the burden of proof and yearn for a level playing field on which to present their arguments. They ask that scholars and others interested in the controversy examine the arguments for both sides and judge which side enjoys the preponderance of evidence.

Leadership for the belief in Will Shakspere's authorship is provided by a handful of senior Shakespearean scholars, perhaps less than a dozen. They believe they are right in their conclusions, even though their arguments may seem less than persuasive to the general reader. At the same time, the Oxfordians have mounted a case for their man that seems to have considerable merit. They have behind them the doubts and dissents about the Stratford man that have been expressed by lawyers and literary figures since the mid-nineteenth century. In the second half of the twentieth century, support for Oxford as the true author has been growing.

As the twenty-first century approaches, Oxford has eclipsed all the other candidates. The growing support for him suggests the need for serious, ongoing inquiry in universities. Trained and supervised scholars should reexamine the traditional belief in Will Shakspere as the author and test the case for Oxford. Archival scholars would find months and years of work to be done in the Public Record Office in London, the Bodleian Library at Oxford, and in mansions that were in the de Vere family. Oxfordians are sure that historical and literary records could yield valuable new information and insights, not just about Oxford and his family but about the men and women around him, from the queen herself to the obscure preacher Francis Meres.

An interdisciplinary study by a university or a humanities foundation could produce valuable results. The authorship issue crosses departmental lines, involving primarily Elizabethan history and English literature, but also comparative literature, English law, art history, and even musicology. (Shakespeare loved music, and Oxford may have been a composer.) Leading scholars in various disciplines could combine their talents.

Universities not only have the talent and the resources for such an interdisciplinary study, they have the mission. They are, in fact, the accepted custodians of the Shakespeare canon and biography. As academic institutions they are also dedicated to intellectual free inquiry and free expression. An interdisciplinary study fits perfectly into the mission of universities. The Oxford challenge to the Bard of Avon deserves serious examination even if it challenges conventional wisdom, perhaps precisely because it does challenge conventional wisdom.

If, perchance, Oxford were determined to be the probable author, a whole new world would open up for scholars and the reading public. Shakespeare's plays and poems would be seen in a new light, and scholars could build new careers explicating the texts in this new light. His biography and the introductions to the plays and poetry would have to be rewritten. Hundreds of scholar-years could be devoted to teasing out and verifying the personal and topical allusions throughout the plays and poems. Young scholars would see great opportunities in researching the volumes of books and papers in archives and libraries. Experienced literary scholars and critics would find irresistible the opportunities for sweeping reevaluations of Shakespeare the poet/dramatist, Shakespeare the chronicler of Elizabethan times,

Shakespeare the supreme commentator on morals and politics, Shakespeare the literary genius of the Elizabethan Age as well as for all time.

The general reader would find Shakespeare more immediately accessible and friendly. The so-called "problem plays" would no longer be so problematic. The *Sonnets* would no longer present so many conundrums. No longer would the author be that strangely self-effacing moneylender, real estate investor, and grain merchant from Stratford-on-Avon, the player who some-how, whether by the miracle of divine inspiration or rewriting the plays of others, or both, gave the world the best dramatic poetry it has ever seen. The plays and poems would take on new meaning, new depth, and heightened emotional significance. Readers of Shakespeare and theatergoers would enjoy a wholly new and enhanced appreciation of the works of Shakespeare.

And Oxford, the man behind the pseudonym Shakespeare, would finally receive the credit for the works he wrote but could not acknowledge as his own. His plea to the world, in the words of the dying Hamlet, would be fulfilled: "Report me and my cause aright to the unsatisfied...tell my story."

All this, if Edward de Vere, seventeenth earl of Oxford, is ac-cepted as the author of the incomparable works that appeared under the name William Shakespeare.

Appendix A

Records of Will Shakspere's Theater Activities

None of the records from Will Shakspere's lifetime that are cited by Stratfordians as evidence of his supposed acting career are theater records. His name, in whatever spelling, does not appear in cast lists, records of payment to actors, or diaries of theater managers. The records cited by Stratfordians are government records, literary allusions, two wills, and a joke.

There are four citations in government documents:

1. In 1595, a record of payment to Will Kemp, Will Shakespeare, and Richard Burbage of the Lord Chamberlain's Men acting company for two performances before the queen. Oxfordians suggest, however, that the record is suspect and possibly fraudulent (Ogburn, 65–66). The court record has the three men acknowledging payment for performances several months earlier, on Innocents Day and St. Stephen's Day, 1594, from the widow of the queen's treasurer. The widow had inherited her late husband's accounts, which were, the queen wrote her, seriously in arrears and due immediately. The widow, moreover, was the mother of the third earl of Southampton, to whom Shakespeare had dedicated the two narrative poems. Small world. Schoenbaum skips this aspect but does note a problem:

"The Innocents Day citation is probably a mistake....The Chamberlain's players seem to have had another date that day. But that is a trifling detail. This record is the first to connect Shakespeare with an acting company, and the *only official notice* [emphasis added] of his name with respect to a theatrical performance" (*Compact Life*, 183). Matus offers another interpretation, suggesting that there was nothing suspect or fraudulent (51ff).

2. In 1602, a handwritten notation on a rejection of a coat of arms for the Shakspere family. The notation, in a different hand from the rest of the document (date unknown), says "Shakespear the Player by Garter," probably disparagingly, since actors' families did not rate coats of arms from the office of the Garter. The documents are reproduced by Schoenbaum in large format and with extensive commentary (*Documentary Life*, 167–73). The *Riverside Shakespeare* (1830–31) provides the key illustration, plus commentary on the documents.

3. In 1603 King James authorized the acting company, including Shakespeare and seven others by name, "to use and exercise the art and faculty of playing comedies, tragedies," and so on (Schoenbaum, *Compact Life*, 250–51).

4. In 1604 Shakespeare, among others of the King's Men acting company, received four and one-half yards of red cloth for a procession (Schoenbaum, *Compact Life*, 251–52).

A lawsuit three years after his death named him as having been a shareholder in the Globe theater at the turn of the century and one of seven men who leased the Blackfriars theater in 1608. His name appears with those of actors, but there is no mention of him being an actor on stage.

Given the complete lack of evidence in the theater records that he was an actor, some Oxfordians question whether there is enough evidence to conclude that Will Shakspere did act on stage in any but the most minor bit parts. Possibly, he was connected with the Lord Chamberlain's Men (later King's Men) acting company in nonacting positions, or perhaps just as a hanger-on. He might then have been known as a "player" simply by virtue of being associated with the company of players. In any case, the silence of the theater records themselves, where his name should have appeared, is highly suggestive.

There are two literary allusions:

1. In 1592 in *Greenes Groatsworth of Wit* and Henry Chettle's apology, convoluted passages that almost defy explication. (See chapter 4 and appendix B.)

2. Around 1610 in a short poem by John Davies, a university student. Davies wrote that Shakespeare played the part of kings. Stratfordian scholars, however, rarely cite this poem as actor evidence, probably because the poem can with equal validity be read as referring to the actor as a nobleman. Since Will Shakspere was not a nobleman, the poem does not work well for Stratfordians (Ogburn, 104). Schoenbaum (*Compact Life*, 200) calls the poem cryptic; Bevington and his predecessor Craig (lxxiv) say only that it apostrophizes Shakespeare; Chute (134) cites only the sixth line, to illustrate his "good temper and instinctive courtesy." Most biographers ignore the poem. It is not discussed by the editors of the *Riverside Shakespeare* or the *Oxford Shakespeare*, or by Bentley, Harrison, Rowse, Fraser, or Kay. The poem, from Davies's *The Scourge of Folly*, is addressed to "Our English Terence, Mr. Will Shake-speare":

> Some say (good Will), which I, in sport, do sing,
> Hadst thou not played some kingly parts in sport,
> Thou hadst been a companion for a king;
> And been a king among the meaner sort.
> Some others rail; but, rail as they think fit,
> Thou hast no railing, but, a reigning wit:
> And honesty thou sowest, which they do reap;
> So, to increase their stock which they do keep.

The two wills are Will Shakspere's own and that of Augustus Phillips. Will Shakspere in 1616 left small bequests, apparently in an afterthought, to three theater friends; and in 1605 Phillips left small bequests in his will to "Shakespeare" and other fellow actors.

The joke was found in a 1602 diary entry written by John Manningham, who had heard it from his roommate. It seems that when Richard Burbage was playing Richard III a woman asked him to meet her that night under that name. Shakespeare overheard the assignation plan and got there first. When Richard III (i.e., Burbage) sent in word that he had arrived, Shakespeare sent back word that William the Conqueror came before Richard III. Manningham then added the information that Shakespeare's name was William, evidently so no one would miss the point of the joke.

Only after Will Shakspere died did the name William Shakespeare appear in theater records. In 1616 Ben Jonson published his *Works*, which listed William Shakespeare among the actors in two of Jonson's plays that had been performed years earlier. They were *Everyman Out of His Humor* and *Sejanus* (Schoenbaum, *Compact Life*, 203). And in 1623 the *First Folio* put Shakespeare's name at the head of the list of the principal players. Ben Jonson's hand in both books raises suspicions for Oxfordians.

Appendix B

"Shake-scene," *Groatsworth*, and Chettle

Greenes Groatsworth of Wit Bought With a Million of Repentence was published in 1592 as the deathbed writing of Robert Greene, poet, playwright, and pamphleteer. Some scholars find evidence that it was written by its publisher, Henry Chettle, who then wrote an apology to those, unnamed, who were offended by it. In his apology Chettle even acknowledged that some thought he, not Greene, had written it. Stratfordian scholars say that *Groatsworth* contains the first allusion to Shakespeare both as an actor and, significantly, as a playwright, although he is not named.

The challenge for the reader is to determine whether the passage in *Groatsworth* about the "upstart crow" who fancies himself a "Shake-scene" and Chettle's apology do indeed provide evidence ("clear" evidence according to most Stratfordian scholars) that Will Shakspere of Stratford-on-Avon was Shakespeare the playwright. If so, it would be the only such reference during his lifetime. Significant background facts:

1. The three unamed playwrights addressed in *Groatsworth* are Marlowe, Nashe, and Peele, according to Stratfordians.

2. The "tiger's heart" line is a parody of a line in *Henry VI Part 3* (1.4.137): "O tiger's heart wrapped in a woman's hide."

3. "Bombast" is read by Oxfordians to mean "fill out" a blank verse. Stratfordians generally take it to mean "stuff out," in other words, "write out" blank verse (*Riverside Shakespeare*, 1835).

4. The *Riverside Shakespeare* also says: "The meaning of 'beautified with our feathers' has been much debated. Some interpret the phrase as an indictment of Shakespeare for plagiarism; others, as merely a reference to Shakespeare as an actor. There is evidence for both views and the matter must be considered unsettled" (1835).

The passage from *Greenes Groatsworth of Wit*:

> Base-minded men all three of you [said to be Marlowe, Nashe, and Peele], if by my misery you not be warned: for unto none of you (like me) sought those burrs to clean: those puppets (I mean) that spake from our mouths, those anticks garnished in our colors. Is it not strange, that I, to whom they all have been beholden: is it not like that you, to whom they all have been beholden, shall (were ye in that case as I am now) be both at once of them forsaken? Yes trust them not: for there is an upstart crow, beautified with our feathers, that with his *tigers heart wrapped in a player's hide*, supposes he is as well able to bombast out a blank verse as the best of you: and being an absolute *Johannes fac totum*, is in his own conceit the only Shake-scene in a country. O that I might entreat your rare wits to be employed in more profitable courses; & let those apes imitate your past excellence, and never more acquaint them with your admired inventions. I know the best husband of you all will never prove a usurer, and the kindest of them all will never prove a kind nurse: yet while you may, seek you better masters; for it is pity men of such rare wits should be subject to the pleasure of such rude grooms.

Later in the same year, Chettle published *Kind Heart's Dream*, which included a letter "To the Gentlemen Readers." The pertinent passage follows:

> About three months since died Mr. Robert Greene, leaving many papers in sundry booksellers' hands, among others

his *Groatsworth of Wit*, in which a letter written to divers play-makers is offensively by one or two of them taken, and because on the dead they cannot be avenged, they willfully forge in their conceits a living author: and after tossing it to and fro, no remedy, but it must light on me. How I have all the time of my conversing in printing hindered the bitter inveighing against scholars, it hath been very well known, and how in that I dealt I can sufficiently prove. With neither of them that take offense was I acquainted, and with one of them I care not if I never be: The other, whom at that time I did not so much spare, as since I wish I had, for that as I have moderated the heat of living writers, and might have made my own discretion (especially in such a case) the author being dead, that I did not, I am as sorry, as if the original fault had been my fault, because myself have seen his demeanor no less civil than he excellent in the quality he professes: Besides, divers of worship* have reported, his uprightness of dealing, which argues his honesty, and his facetious grace in writing, that proves his art.

*Men of high social standing.

Appendix C

Ben Jonson's Notebook, *Timber*

Timber, or Discoveries, Made Upon Men and Matter, from the notebooks of Ben Jonson, was never published by Jonson. His notebooks were found after his death in 1637, fourteen years after publication of the *First Folio* and twenty-one years after Will Shakspere died. (Alden Brooks devoted a 135-page book, *This Side of Shakespeare* [New York: Vantage, 1964], to a curious, intense analysis of the five-paragraph passage.)

The challenge for the reader is to decide to what extent Ben Jonson approves of Shakespeare, whoever he was. The excerpt from *Timber*:

> Nothing in our age, I have observed, is more preposterous than the running judgements upon poetry and poets; when we shall hear those things commended and cried up for the best writings, which a man would scarce vouchsafe to wrap any wholesome drug in; he would never light his tobacco with them. And those men almost named for miracles, who yet are so vile, that if a man should go about to examine, and correct them, he must make all they have done, but one blot. Their good is so entangled with their bad, as forcibly one must draw on the other's death with it. A sponge dipped in ink will do all.

Yet their vices have not hurt them: nay, a great many they have profited; for they have been loved for nothing else. And this false opinion grows strong against the best men; if once it take root with the ignorant.

Jonson goes on in this vein for three paragraphs, complaining about popular judgments of poets and poetry and about the ignorance of the "sordid multitudes." The section of his notebook concludes with a paragraph that is marked in Latin "About our Shakespeare":

I remember the players have often mentioned it as an honor to Shakespeare, that in his writing (whatsoever he penned) he never blotted out a line. My answer hath been, would he had blotted a thousand. Which they thought a malevolent speech. I had not told posterity this, but for their ignorance, who choose that circumstance to commend their friend by, wherein he most faulted. And to justify mine own candor, (for I loved the man, and do honor his memory (on this side idolatry) as much as any). He was (indeed) honest, and of an open, and free nature; had an excellent phantasy; brave notions, and gentle expressions: wherein he flowed with that facility, that sometimes it was necessary he should be stopped: *Sufflaminandus erat**; as Augustus said of Haterius. His wit was in his own power; would the rule of it had been so too. Many times he fell into those things, could not escape laughter; as when he said in the person of Caesar, one speaking to him, "Caesar, thou dost me wrong." He replied: "Caesar did never wrong, but with just cause" and such like; which were ridiculous. But he redeemed his vices with his virtues. There was ever more in him to be praised, than to be pardoned.

*"He needed a drag-chain" (presumably to make him slow down and stop).

Appendix D

The Benezet Test

The following seventy-one lines were selected by Professor Louis P. Benezet* from Shakespeare's writings and from Oxford's poetry, which was written in his early years. No passage is longer than eight lines, none shorter than four. Six are from the works attributed to one author; seven from the other. Judging solely by the intrinsic literary quality and characteristics, and without referring to any texts, who wrote which passages? Although the test does not prove that Oxford wrote Shakespeare, it does show that in his early years he wrote poetry that was remarkably similar in voice and generally of the same quality.

> If care or skill could conquer vain desire,
> Or reason's reins my strong affections stay:
> There should my sighs to quiet breast retire,
> And shun such sights as secret thoughts betray;
> Uncomely love which now lurks in my breast
> Should cease, my grief by wisdom's power oppressed.
> My reason, the physician to my love,
> Angry that his prescriptions are not kept,
> Hath left me, and I desperate now approve
> Desire is death, which physic did except.
> Past cure I am, now reason is past care,

And frantic mad with evermore unrest.
Fain would I sing, but fury makes me fret,
And rage hath sworn to seek revenge of wrong;
My mazed mind in malice is so set,
As death shall daunt my deadly dolours long;
Patience perforce is such a pinching pain,
As die I will or suffer wrong again.
For, if I should despair, I should go mad,
And in my madness might speak ill of thee:
Now this ill-wrestling world has grown so bad,
Mad slanderers by mad ears believed be.
Love is a discord and a strange divorce
Betwixt our sense and rest; by whose power,
As mad with reason we admit that force
Which wit or labour never may endower.
My thoughts and my discourse as madmen's are,
As random from the truth vainly express'd;
For I have sworn thee fair and thought thee bright
Who art as black as hell and dark as night.
Why should my heart think that a several plot
Which my heart knows the wide world's common place?
Or mine eyes seeing this, say this is not,
To put fair truth upon so foul a face?
Who taught thee first to sigh, alas, my heart?
Who taught thy tongue the woeful words of plaint?
Who filled your eyes with tears of bitter smart?
Who gave thee grief and made thy joys to faint?
Who first did paint with colours pale thy face?
Who first did break thy sleeps of quiet rest?
Above the rest in court who gave thee grace?
Who made thee strive in honour to be best?
Who taught thee how to make me love thee more
The more I hear and see just cause of hate?
O, though I love what others do abhor,
With others thou shouldst not abhor my state:
What worldly wight can hope for heavenly hire,
When only sighs must make his secret moan:
A silent suit doth seld to grace aspire,
My hapless hap doth roll the restless stone.

Yet Phoebe fair disdained the heavens above,
To 'joy on earth her poor Endymion's love.
And shall I live on earth to be her thrall?
And shall I live and serve her all in vain?
And shall I kiss the steps that she lets fall?
And shall I pray the gods to keep the pain
From her that is so cruel still?
No, no, on her work all your will.
And let her feel the power of all your might,
And let her have her most desire with speed,
And let her pine away both day and night,
And let moan and none lament her need;
And let all those that shall her see,
Despise her state and pity me.
Let him have time to tear his curled hair,
Let him have time against himself to rave,
Let him have time of Time's help to despair,
Let him have time to live a loathed slave,
Let him have time a beggar's orts to crave,
And time to see one that by alms doth live
Disdain to him disdained scraps to give.

*Proposed by the late Professor Louis P. Benezet of Dartmouth College in *Shakspere, Shakespere and de Vere* (Manchester, NH: Granite State Press, 1937).

PREFACE

1. *Life* magazine article by Dora Jane Hamblin, April 23, 1964; see also *Life* editorial, September 7, 1962, by John K. Jessup (cited by Ogburn, 148, 171, 182).

CHAPTER 1: A STRIKINGLY MUNDANE LIFE

1. By "world's greatest" poet/dramatist is meant the most widely appreciated, most extensively studied, and most influential. The dramatists of ancient Greece and Rome may be esteemed by some as both earlier in time and greater in genius. Shakespeare, however, has probably influenced more readers and theatergoers in more important ways than any other poet/dramatist (Taylor, 377; and Michael H. Hart, *The 100: A Ranking of the Most Influential Persons in History* [New York: Citadel, 1992, chap. 31]).

2. Some biographers deny any dilemma. They adopt an air of confident assertion, coupled with coy disclaimers, which sometimes approach epidemic proportions. In the earlier Folger Library editions (1958), Louis B. Wright rejected any doubts that the Stratford man was the author, but then thirteen times in seven short pages resorted to "probably" (four times), "perhaps," "undoubtedly," "surmise," "may have," and the like; and he still found space to mention four legends, such as that Will Shakspere was a deer poacher. Sylvan Barnet uses five "perhaps" to qualify significant matters in his four-page biography in the Signet editions (1987).

3. Sources for quotations on pages 3–6 are the following: George Saintsbury, *A Short History of English Literature* (New York: Macmillan, 1935, 315); George Sampson, *Concise Cambridge History of English Literature*, 3d ed., rev. by R. C. Churchill (Cambridge: Cambridge University Press, 1970, 214). Eagleton's review was in the British newspaper *The Independent* of November 6, 1991. Dawson's quote is from *The Life of William Shakespeare* (Washington, DC: Folger Shakespeare Library, 1958, 1). Dawson's colleagues are Barbara A. Mowat of the Folger and Professor Paul Werstine, who wrote the introduction to *The New Folger Library Shakespeare* (xxxiii). George Lyman Kittredge, *Shakspere: An Address*, delivered on April 23, 1916, in Sanders Theater at the request of the president and fellows of Harvard College (Cambridge: Harvard University Press, 1916, 9, 46). The *Oxford Shakespeare* (xix), Rowse (1), Chute (ix), Barnet (vii), Schoenbaum, *Shakespeare: His Life, His Language, His Theater* (New York: Penguin, 1990, 14–15), Bevington (lxi), Epstein (21), Harrison (3–5).

4. Ralph Waldo Emerson, *Representative Men* (Boston: Phillips, Sampson, 1850, 214–15). See also Hope and Holston, 152–53.

5. Will Shakspere's father signed with a mark and left no example of any writing. For conventional scholars, what this means ranges from "absolute illiteracy" (James O. Halliwell-Phillipps, *Outline of the Life of Shakespeare* [London: Longman's, 1887, 24] to "he never learned to write" (Rowse, *The Man*, 15) to "apparently John himself could not write" (Schoenbaum, *Lives*, 8) to "he must have had some education" (Craig, 72) to "his financial aptitude and ready command of figures satisfactorily relieve him of the imputation of illiteracy" (Lee, 6).

6. No records exist to show that Will Shakspere ever went to school, but that has not deterred biographers. Fraser (1:57) states flatly that he "took his place in school at the age of four or five" and devotes fifteen full pages of description to it. Rowse (*The Man*, 19) is equally confident: "In fact, he had the regular grammar-school education of the day." Chute (14) has him "learning his letters from the parish clerk...and as soon as he could read and write and knew his Catechism, young William Shakespeare was ready to enter Stratford grammar school." Schoenbaum (*Lives*, 67) cautiously opines that "there is every likelihood that the future poet studied there." Wright (xxvi) declares, "Though the records are lost, there can be no reason to doubt that this is where young William Shakespeare received his education." Montague (133) says "it is just inconceivable that he did not send his eldest son, William Shakespeare, to the school." Craig (73) goes so far as to call the grammar school curriculum "as adequately educational as any four-year college," but without explaining how in rural England in the 1570s this could be so. It's all extrapolation: Stratford had a grammar school, ergo the future poet must have studied there, and this is what it must have been like.

7. The sparse and scattered records of Will Shakspere's theater activities are listed in appendix A. Schoenbaum in *Documentary Life* and Chambers provide full details of the legal, church, and theater records of his life; Ogburn offers a useful summary analysis in chapter 3.

8. Schoenbaum's lament about the "sublimity of the subject" versus "the mundane inconsequence of the documentary record" (*Lives*, 568) echoes J. Dover Wilson in *The Essential Shakespeare* (2): "The sublimity of the subject, and the comparative poverty of contemporary information about it, expose anyone who undertakes to write a life of Shakespeare to many perils, but the greatest of them all is the personal equation."

CHAPTER 2: THE MISSING LITERARY EVIDENCE

1. Michael Drayton was born near Stratford a year after Will Shakspere. Prominent in the theater, he collaborated with others on at least twenty plays for London acting companies. Francis Meres mentioned him thirteen times, to six for Shakespeare (Bentley, chap. 8). Yet the record is bare of any communication between the two or any word by Drayton about his neighbor. Eleven years after Will Shakspere died, Drayton wrote a four-line poem addressed to Shakespeare (C. M. Ingleby et al., *The Shakspere Allusion Book* [London: The New Shakspere Society, 1909]).

2. No letters sent or received by Will Shakspere have been found. Business and personal letters might not have been saved for posterity, but literary letters, if there were any, should have had a better chance of survival. One business letter addressed to him did survive, but it evidently was never delivered. It was written by Richard Quiney of Stratford asking for a loan, but it was found in Quiney's papers, with no indication that it had ever been sent (*Riverside Shakespeare*, 1832; Chambers, 2:101).

3. A handwritten fragment in a manuscript of the play *Sir Thomas More* has been attributed to Shakespeare by some Stratfordian scholars, who also consider it his own handwriting; but others are doubtful (Schoenbaum, *Compact Life*, 214–17, 320). Neither Bevington (lxvii) nor the *Oxford Shakespeare* (785) judge the merits. The *Riverside Shakespeare* treats the possibility at length, but only as a possibility: "If Hand D is Shakespeare's" (1683–84). Ogburn cites evidence undercutting the theory (122–23, 676).

4. A possible seventh signature is described in the *Shakespeare Quarterly* (Spring 1992) by Giles Dawson, emeritus curator at the Folger Library. It appears on the edge of a page of a book by Lambarde, acquired by the Folger in 1938. Some consider it a forgery (Miller, 2:329–38).

5. The authenticity of the three signatures on the will was questioned in 1985 by Jane Cox, custodian of the will in the Public Record Office in London. In a booklet, *Shakespeare's Will and Signatures*, published by Her Majesty's Stationery Office, she points out that the signatures of three witnesses "are suspiciously similar" and that, moreover, it was not unusual for clerks to transcribe wills, including even the signatures. She also notes that literate men of the time "developed personalized signatures...it is unthinkable Shakespeare did not." In a postscript to his *Compact Life*, Schoenbaum allows that "a sceptical inquirer has made necessary a re-examination of comfortable assumptions" (327).

6. On Will Shakspere shunning the spotlight, see Kay (7), Rowse (*The Man*, 234), and Fraser (4).

7. The inscription on the monument opens with two lines in Latin comparing the deceased to Nestor, Socrates, and Virgil. Neither Nestor nor Socrates wrote anything. Ogburn notes that Sophocles, the Greek dramatist, would have been more appropriate than Socrates, the philosopher, and that Ovid, who influenced Shakespeare most, would have been better than Virgil (214). The English inscription reads:

Stay, passenger, why goest thou by so fast?
Read if thou canst, whom envious death hath plast
Within this monument Shakspeare: with whom
Quick nature died: whose name doth deck this tomb,
Far more than cost: since all that he hath writ,
Leaves living art, but page, to serve his wit.

8. Biographers date the Stratford monument to sometime in the seven years after Will Shakspere's death because the first mention of a monument is in the *First Folio* (1623), although that mention is ambiguous. Schoenbaum (*Compact Life*, 313) surmises, as do other Stratfordians, that Sir William Dugdale, the publisher, simply "misrepresents the subject." That would require that Dugdale somehow forgot or deliberately omitted the pen and paper in a monument ostensibly to an author. Ogburn (210) gives a history and illustrations of both engravings. Curiously, Craig's *Complete Works of Shakespeare* includes only the early grain-dealer engraving (69) but without comment, then follows a thousand pages later (1150) with a single sentence: "To what extent it [the monument] was tampered with at a later time is not certain." And Craig's edition unaccountably fails to show the reader what the monument and bust look like today.

9. The quarto editions of the plays came first; half the plays appeared individually in quarto editions. The *First Folio* came later, after Shakespeare's death. It was the first collected edition of the plays; second, third, and fourth editions, or folios, followed. The terms quarto and folio derive from the way sheets of printing paper were folded after printing, folio pages making a much larger and more substantial book.

10. Bentley says Will Shakspere might well have acted in fifty or sixty plays a year: "Such training was very strenuous" (93). Taylor's opening sentences (3) describe how Will Shakspere "might be expected to perform in six different plays on six consecutive days," rehearsing in the morning and performing in the afternoon; Taylor adds that "when he was not acting in plays he was writing them." Neither author explains how Will Shakspere found the time and energy to act, to learn all he

had to learn, and then write the poems and plays, and run his businesses, too.

11. For his Warwickshire accent and dialect, see Miller (2:283–86).

12. The circumstances of the publication of *Shake-speares Sonnets* are covered in detail by Ogburn (chap. 17) and Ogburn and Ogburn (75ff.). Schoenbaum (*Compact Life*, 268ff.) says scholars find the circumstances "vexing" and the dedication "mystifying." Bevington (1612) says, "Probably no puzzle in all English literature has provoked so much speculation and produced so little agreement." Robert Giroux, in *The Story of Q* (New York: Random House, 1982), calls the *Sonnets* one of the most mysterious books in the history of publishing. At its appearance it was totally ignored and probably suppressed. A second edition did not appear for more than a century. Several biographers, including Rowse and Fraser, simply ignore the puzzle; Chute relegates the *Sonnets* to an appendix. Stratfordian authorities are divided on whether the *Sonnets* are autobiographical (*Riverside Shakespeare*, 1748; Bevington, 1614).

13. Like the *Sonnets*, *Venus and Adonis* and *The Rape of Lucrece* carry no byline on the title page, where the author's name would usually be found. A curious omission. Shakespeare's name only appears on the dedications following the title pages.

CHAPTER 3: SHAKSPERE VERSUS SHAKESPEARE

1. For the hundred spellings and additional detail, see B. Roland Lewis, *The Shakespeare Documents: Facsimiles, Transliterations, Translations and Commentary*, 2 vols. (Stanford, CA: Stanford University Press, 1940); also Chambers (appendix E), and Ogburn (92).

2. Partial exceptions to the Shakespeare spelling occur in two of the ten quartos that carry the author's name. Title pages of the ten plays are reproduced in *The Reader's Encyclopedia of Shakespeare* (New York: Crowell, 1966). The *Love's Labour's Lost* quarto (1598), the first with the author's name on it, spelled it Shakespere, which, however, is not a Stratfordian, flat "a" variation. The *King Lear* quarto of 1608 spelled it Shak-speare, but in 1619 the same play was printed with a new title page, backdated 1608, that changed (corrected?) the name to Shake-speare. A Revels Account document records the playwright's name as Shaxberd, but the entries have been challenged as a nineteenth-century forgery (Schoenbaum, *Documentary Life*, 200, citing Samuel A. Tannenbaum, *Shakespeare Forgeries in the Revels Account*, 1928). Oddly, the only major deviation from the uniform pattern is the handwritten entry in the Stationers Register (1623) for the *First Folio*, which spelled the name Shakspeer(e?). See Schoenbaum's *Documentary Life* (257). But then in the

same year the *First Folio* itself spelled it uniformly Shakespeare and Shake-speare throughout, nineteen times in all.

3. *The Shakspere Allusion Book, 1591–1700*, ed. John Munro (London: The New Shakspere Society, 1909) provides transcriptions of allusions to Shakespeare and his works, including the various spellings of the name.

4. Both spellings, Shakespeare and Shakspere, were used to refer to a poet/dramatist in parts of the three satirical Parnassus plays (1598–1602), but mockingly and in disbelief, evidently to express skepticism that Will Shakspere was the author (Ogburn, 106). Stratfordian biographers do not make much of the references in the Parnassus plays. When they do mention them, they describe them simply as innocent fun, harmlessly equivocal. Bevington calls them a "backhanded tribute" to the author (lxiv); Schoenbaum, "back-handed recognition" (*Compact Life*, 177). See also Kay (159). The *Riverside Shakespeare* (1837–38) provides the texts and footnote comments so readers can decide for themselves whether the scenes and the spellings prove anything about authorship.

5. For hyphenation, see Ogburn (96–98). The name was hyphenated on fifteen quartos, not hyphenated on nineteen; see Percy Allen, *The Oxford-Shakespeare Case Corroborated* (London: Palmer, 1931, 5). Matus questions the significance of hyphenation (chapter 2).

6. The Shakespeare spelling and *its* variants (i.e., with the long "a"), were used for the name of the man from Stratford in a third of about sixty-five documents, including the applications for a coat of arms (Schoenbaum, *Documentary Life*, 166–73; Ogburn, 28). By far the most common spellings for the Stratford man were the variants Shakspere, Shaksper, and Shackspeare.

7. The six signatures on four documents are reproduced in the *Riverside Shakespeare* (1696) along with facsimile pages of the *Sir Thomas More* manuscript thought by some to be in the author's hand. See also Ogburn (119–23).

8. The Shakspere/Shakespeare name, ranging from Shaxper to Schackeschafte, was common in Elizabethan times. It is conceivable that some of the legal records refer to someone other than the man from Stratford, although no significant conflicts or inconsistencies have been found.

9. Good name and honor are recurring themes in Shakespeare. Dying, Hamlet says: "Oh, God, Horatio, what a wounded name, things standing thus unknown, shall live behind me" (5.2.344–5). All quotations from Shakespeare's works are from the *Riverside Shakespeare*. In the *Sonnets*, see, for example, numbers 36, 72, 76, 81, and 111.

10. On modernizing the spelling, Professor Stanley Wells, an experienced Shakespeare editor, warns: "Anyone who has himself attempted
to modernize the spelling of an Elizabethan author in a responsible fashion is likely to know that in fact it calls for many delicate decisions"
(*Modernizing Shakespeare's Spelling* [Oxford: Oxford University Press,
1979, 3]). See also Chute (xii).

11. For Furnivall's quote, see *Shakspere Allusion Book* (6). In the twentieth century, Professor George Lyman Kittredge, the eminent Harvard
Shakespearean, insisted on the Shakspere spelling, according to E. J.
Kahn, Jr., who was there (*About the New Yorker and Me* [New York:
Penguin, 1979, 327]). And even Gibson, a defender of the Stratfordian
faith, says the use of the Shakspere spelling "is convenient to make a
distinction and avoid ambiguity." (14).

CHAPTER 4: THE CASE FOR WILL SHAKSPERE AS AUTHOR

For full-scale studies of the traditional belief that the man from Stratford wrote Shakespeare, see Schoenbaum's *Lives* and his *Documentary
Life* in the large or compact edition, the most fully documented of the
biographies; also Ogburn (especially chaps. 2, 9); Taylor; and Brown and
Fearon.

1. The three unreliable writers of biographical notes in the seventeenth century were Thomas Fuller, the Rev. John Ward, and John Aubrey. Fuller's *Worthies* (1662) has only a few sentences; and Ward, vicar
of the Stratford church in the 1660s, left four sentences in his diary, not
published until 1839 (Schoenbaum, *Documentary Life*, 155, 207). Ogburn
notes that Ward's diary can be read to argue *against* Will Shakspere as
the author (18). Aubrey, an antiquarian and gossipmonger, wrote a
short, anecdotal biography that was not published until 1813 in a book
entitled *Brief Lives*. These three, plus Rowe's error-filled sketch in 1709,
were the only attempts at biography until the nineteenth century. The
late-eighteenth-century Shakespearean, Edmund Malone, counted
eleven biographical facts in Rowe's biography and found eight of them
to be wrong (Schoenbaum, *Lives*, 169).

2. The clergyman investigator was the Rev. James Wilmot, rector of
a village near Stratford-on-Avon. In the 1780s he confided to a friend
his conclusion that Will Shakspere did not write the plays and poems,
but Wilmot would not allow publication of his findings. His work only
came to light in 1932, a century and a half later (Ogburn, 126–28).

3. The two forgers were William-Henry Ireland and John Payne Col-
lier. Both are covered extensively by Schoenbaum in *Lives* (part 3: chap-

ters 8 and 9; part 4: chapters 10 and 11) and in his descriptions of various documents in *Documentary Life*.

4. The Stratford monument and the *First Folio* are usually the principal historical evidence cited to counter questions about Will Shakspere's authorship. The *Concise Oxford Companion to English Literature* (Oxford: Oxford University Press, 1990, 511) says that any doubts "are best answered by the facts that the monument to William Shakespeare of Stratford-on-Avon compares him with Socrates and Virgil and that Jonson's verses in the *First Folio* identify the author of that volume as the 'Sweet Swan of Avon.' "

5. Harry Levin, *Shakespeare and the Revolution of the Times* (Oxford: Oxford University Press, 1976, 319); the book includes a reprint of Levin's article, written in collaboration with G. Blakemore Evans, in *Harvard Magazine*, February 1975).

6. The text from *Groatsworth* and Chettle's apology are given in appendix B. See also Ogburn's interpretation (chap. 5).

7. Ogburn (chapter 5) describes the persuasive evidence that Chettle almost certainly wrote *Groatsworth*. Chettle himself said he transcribed it for the typesetters. Textual analysis says it is in Chettle's style. (See Miller [2:340].)

8. The cryptic Shake-scene allusion in *Groatsworth*, central to Stratfordian belief, seized the imagination of the editors of the widely used high school text *England in Literature* (Glenview, IL: Scott, Foresman, 1989). More than a third of the one-page biography is devoted to the allusion in Groatsworth (185). Schoenbaum devotes eleven pages to it (*Compact Life*, 147–58). Rowse calls the Shake-scene allusion "a timebomb which has gone on reverberating ever since" (*Biography*, 97).

9. During the thirty-one years between the Shake-scene allusion and the *First Folio*, there were some fifty literary references to Shakespeare's poems and plays. Two of them, the Parnassus plays and a short poem by "F. B." to Ben Jonson (c. 1608–15), are sometimes cited as testimony to authorship by the Stratford man, but both present problems of interpretation. Neither is cited regularly by Stratfordians. For the Parnassus plays, see chapter 3. The poet "F. B." was probably Francis Beaumont. Stratfordians interpret two lines about Shakespeare's "dim light of Nature" in the poem as an allusion to the relatively uneducated Will Shakspere. Ogburn, however, discovered that some Stratfordians were using a falsified text and that the original conveys the opposite meaning (Ogburn, 109; *Riverside Shakespeare*, 1845; Schoenbaum, *Lives*, 27). Once again, identification of Shakespeare is based on an elusive allusion.

10. The monument's inscription is almost totally ignored by Stratfordians. Biographies in Harrison, the *Riverside Shakespeare*, and the *Oxford*

Shakespeare make no comment on it; Bevington (lxxvi) only on the Latin. Lee (497) and Levi (343) each offer a single, short paragraph. Schoenbaum (*Lives*, 310) omits any comment on the text, except to note a possible mistake in one word, "sieh." Also omitting any comment are Bentley, Wilson, Chute, Brown, and Fraser; Rowse only calls them "rather good funerary verses (*Biography*, 454). For the text, see the notes to chapter 2.

    11. Allusions in Shakespeare's works that might seem to refer to Will Shakspere are mostly general and vague. F. E. Halliday writes, for example, in his *Life of Shakespeare* (Baltimore: Penguin, 1962, 127) that *The Taming of the Shrew* is "full of allusions to his Stratford neighborhood": Sly was born in the home town of a cousin of Will Shakspere; he haunts an alehouse near Stratford; a troupe of traveling players passes through. Schoenbaum (*Compact Life*, 74) quotes E. I. Fripp on Shakespeare's knowledge of the leather-working trade, that of Will Shakspere's father. Fraser sprinkles his two-volume biography with hundreds of very brief quotations from the plays, subtly leaving an impression that Will Shakspere's life was everywhere reflected in the plays; for example, there are five allusions on one page (1:57) about his imagined schooling. Caroline F. E. Spurgeon in *Shakespeare's Imagery* (Cambridge: Cambridge University Press, 1935, 98) picks as her favorite a river's eddy under an arch described in the *Rape of Lucrece* (lines 1667–73). Her frontispiece is her own sketch of the Stratford bridge showing with arrows "the movement of the current with the eddy in front." In *Merry Wives of Windsor* the character Shallow has "luces" in his coat of arms, a possible reference to Sir Thomas Lucy, in whose game park, according to legend. Will Shakspere is supposed to have poached. Rowse and Fraser, among others, quote from *As You Like It* about the "whining schoolboy with his satchel, and shining morning face, creeping like a snail unwillingly to school," behavior that Will Shakspere would have seen in Stratford. Chambers, the eminent Stratfordian scholar, notes what is perhaps the best candidate: "Possibly the drowning of a Katherine Hamlet at Tiddington on the Avon in 1579 [Will was 13] may have given a hint for Ophelia's end. All this amounts to very little. Whatever imprint Shakespeare's Warwickshire contemporaries may have left upon his imagination eludes us" (25). Kay laments: "There are not, alas, many local references in Shakespeare's plays" (65).

CHAPTER 5: THE AMBIGUOUS TESTIMONY OF THE *FIRST FOLIO*

1. How the *First Folio* was printed has been analyzed in meticulous detail by Charlton K. Hinman and Peter W. M. Blayney in *The First Folio of Shakespeare* (Washington, DC: Folger Shakespeare Library, 1991).

2. All the opening pages of the *First Folio* are reproduced in the *Riverside Shakespeare* (58ff.).

3. Ben Jonson was the first writer to publish his own "collected works" (David Riggs, *Ben Jonson: A Life* [Cambridge: Harvard University Press, 1989, 220ff.]).

4. Leonard Digges's connections with Stratford-on-Avon were discovered by Leslie Hotson, who found that Digges from age twelve had been raised by his stepfather at Alderminster, near Stratford-on-Avon (*I, William Shakespeare* [London: Oxford University Press, 1937, chap. 10]).

5. The "Not Without Mustard" line appears in Ben Jonson's satirical comedy *Every Man Out of His Humour*. The jibe is aimed at a rustic clown named Sogliardo, who is ridiculed as someone "so enamoured of the name of a gentleman that he will have it though he buys it." In Jonson's poem "Epigram 56" he accuses an unnamed "poet-ape" of trying to take credit for plays written by someone else. The pertinent lines in the play and the poem are quoted by Miller (2:44ff.), also by Chambers (vol. 2). In both allusions the butt of the ridicule, unnamed, could be Will Shakspere or someone else.

6. The Scots poet who recorded his conversations with Ben Jonson was William Drummond, whom Jonson visited in 1618, two years after Will Shakspere's death. Stratfordian biographers of Shakespeare rarely cite the disparaging reference. Ogburn gives the text (219).

7. On the peculiar nature of the portrait engraving and portrait poem, see Ogburn (224). Of course, Ben Jonson in his denigrating poem opposite the portrait could have been simply saying "terrible portrait, doesn't look much like him." But that raises questions about why it was commissioned to portray the man Jonson praised so highly in his memorial poem four pages later.

8. Ben Jonson's portrait poem and the title page are also judged to be quite odd by Professor Leah Marcus, a Stratfordian and new historicist critic. She contrasts the opening pages of the *First Folio* with those of similar, contemporary works. The engraving, she writes, has an "unsettling size and directness"; it is "stark and unadorned" with no frame, ornamental borders, allegorical figures, or other embellishments usually found on such title pages. The portrait in its "raw directness" seems to

say "this is the Man Himself." But, Marcus continues, "the verses on the facing page say otherwise." The portrait poem "undermines the visual power of the portrait" and destabilizes it. In her view, "Jonson's poem abolishes Shakespeare as an entity apart from his writings" (*Puzzling Shakespeare* [Berkeley: University of California Press, 1988, 2–25]). Marcus includes facsimiles of typical title pages from other works and a consideration of non-Stratfordian explanations. The *First Folio* is dramatically plain compared to other books of the time.

9. Various other supposed portraits of Shakespeare are used in biographies and textbooks and with editions of Shakespeare's works. The so-called Chandos, Janssen, and Ashbourne portraits have been the most popular. None has undisputed title to be the authentic portrait of Shakespeare (see Schoenbaum, *Lives*, 202–14).

10. Conventional scholarship sees no ambiguity in the line "small Latin and less Greek," although the main alternate reading has been cited for more than a hundred years (Ogburn, 232). In an unpublished paper, Andrew Hannas of Purdue University has suggested the second alternate reading.

11. Among the leading Stratfordian scholars who agree that Ben Jonson, not Heminge and Condell, probably wrote the two dedicatory letters in the *First Folio* are Steevens, Malone, and Chambers (Ogburn, 226). Schoenbaum is silent on the issue.

12. For "sweet swan of Avon" as referring also to Oxford's Bilton estate, see Miller (2:355–69), Ogburn (235, 713).

13. For "thy Stratford moniment" see Ogburn (13, 236). Miller analyzes "monument" and "moniment" in an unpublished paper delivered February 24, 1990, at the Pasadena Public Library.

14. Burial arrangements apparently inspired a student at Oxford to write a short poem. Sometime between Will Shakspere's death and publication of the *First Folio*, William Basse, the student, wrote a poem entitled: "On Mr. Wm. Shakespeare. He died in April 1616." Basse calls on Chaucer, Spenser, and Beaumont, who were honored by burial in Westminster Abbey, to move closer and make room for Shakespeare in their tomb (*Riverside Shakespeare*, 1845). Although the poem was not printed until 1633, Ben Jonson apparently saw the manuscript. His memorial poem in the *First Folio* of 1623 squelches the idea:

> My Shakespeare, rise; I will not lodge thee by
> Chaucer, or Spenser, or bid Beaumont lie
> A little further to make thee a room.
> Thou art a moniment, without a tomb,
> And art alive still, while thy book doth live,
> And we have wits to read, and praise to give.

Miller (2:31) notes that Basse, like Ben Jonson, was closely associated with Oxford's daughters, who would not have wanted Will Shakspere's body moved to Westminster Abbey.

CHAPTER 6: THE SEARCH FOR THE TRUE AUTHOR

This chapter draws principally on Ogburn, Schoenbaum (*Lives*), Looney, and Hope and Holston's "Chronological Annotated Bibliography."

1. John Adams's notes on his visit to Stratford-on-Avon are quoted in Hope and Holston (151) from the *Diary and Autobiography of John Adams*.

2. See Ogburn (126) on *The Story of the Learned Pig*; see Hope and Holston (149–50) and Miller (2:244–48) for excerpts from the earlier allegory and literary essay.

3. On the Rev. Wilmot, see Ogburn (126–28), Hope and Holston (151, 181).

4. For quotations from Disraeli, Hart, Emerson, Whittier, Whitman, and James, see Hope and Holston.

5. For quotations from Twain, see his *Is Shakespeare Dead* (New York and London: Harper & Brothers, 1909, 11–16). Twain drew heavily on writings of Sir G. George Greenwood, a lawyer and author of *The Shakespeare Problem Restated* (1908). Greenwood is one of the most respected critics of the case for Will Shakspere as author.

6. For biographies of Looney, see Hope and Holston (chap. 7), and Miller (appendix V, 1:648). Although his critics made fun of his name, Looney held it in high regard and made no apologies for it. In fact, he said that he lost his first publisher because he refused to agree to use a pseudonym. It would have been ironic for Looney to have used a pseudonym on a book about his discovery of the man behind the most famous pseudonym in history (Miller, 1:xxx; Ogburn, 376).

7. For Cooper and Galsworthy, see the "Afterwords" by Charles Wisner Barrell to the 1949 U.S. edition of Looney (454–55); also Hope and Holston (178). On Freud, see Miller (2:264–73), Hope and Holston (184).

8. The reader of Ward's biography of Oxford who is not forewarned may at first be puzzled by the lack of references to Looney's book and to the proposition that Oxford wrote Shakespeare. Ward provides no explanation at the start of his book. Only on page 328 does he briefly explain that he considered it outside the scope of his biography to treat "controversial matters that cannot be definitely settled by contemporary documents and evidence." Ward was well aware of Looney's work, which led him to undertake the five years of research that was required

for the biography. In it, however, he limited his purview to contemporary records of Oxford's life that he found in the archives.

CHAPTER 7: OXFORD'S LITERARY LIFE

Bernard M. Ward's biography of Oxford (1928) remains the most comprehensive scholarly work, and this chapter draws heavily on it. A short biography of Oxford, quite outdated but still illuminating in the context of its time and authorship, can be found in the *Dictionary of National Biography* (DNB). It was written by Sir Sidney Lee in the late nineteenth century before Oxford became a candidate as Shakespeare. Ironically, Lee also wrote the DNB biography of Shakespeare (i.e., Will Shakspere), and became the leading Shakespearean biographer of his day. Doubly ironic is the fact that Lee's name was itself not his original name.

1. A vivid, imaginative portrayal of Oxford's arrival in London at age twelve is provided by Ogburn and Ogburn in the opening pages of their book.

2. On wardship and its perils, see Joel Hurtsfield, *The Queen's Wards* (London: Longman's Green, 1958, 81, 241–51), quoted by Clark (111–13).

3. On Oxford's "fray," see Miller (2:84) and Ward (227).

4. Schoenbaum (*Lives*, 432) cannot resist quoting an anecdote from Aubrey: "The Earl of Oxford, making of his low obeisance to Queen Elizabeth, happened to let a fart, at which he was so ashamed that he went to travel, 7 years." Oxfordians usually let this pass unnoticed. Schoenbaum allows that it is probably apocryphal, but adds in a footnote that the episode "has escaped the noses of Oxfordians."

5. For Oxford's poems, as compiled by Looney with comments, see Miller (appendix III). Ogburn notes that Professor Steven W. May questions the attribution of some of them, accepting sixteen as by Oxford (396).

6. For Oxford as playwright and patron of writers, see Ward (179–205).

7. Oxford in his early thirties was accused by a political enemy of homosexual activity and indulging in "all kinds of vice and shameful treacheries." Ogburn notes that the accusation came from a man Oxford had exposed as a traitor (342, 644). Oxford had at least six children by two wives and a mistress.

8. Testimony to Oxford's excellence as a playwright in Webbe and in *The Art of English Poesy* (by Puttenham?) came during Oxford's lifetime; in 1622, Henry Peacham wrote that among those who "honored Poesie with their pens and practice...were Edward Earl of Oxford" (Miller, 1:559, 2:310; Ogburn, 687).

9. Curiously, the sum of one thousand pounds, which Oxford received annually from the treasury, turned up decades later, not once but twice, in accounts about Will Shakspere of Stratford. In the 1660s the Rev. John Ward, vicar of the Stratford church, wrote in his notebook that Shakespeare "supplied the stage with 2 plays every year, and for that had an allowance so large that he spent at the rate of 1000 pounds a year, as I have heard" (Ogburn, 19). The spending rate is too enormous to be believed by any scholars, but for some reason Ward linked playwriting to the sum of one thousand pounds. The amount was very roughly a hundred times what a teacher in Stratford earned. Forty years later Nicholas Rowe, in his introduction to the works of Shakespeare, wrote that "Southampton, at one time, gave him a thousand pounds, to enable him to go through with a purchase which he heard he had a mind to. A bounty very great and very rare at any time" (Ogburn, 194). Still an enormous sum even for a one-time gift, but Rowe, too, for some reason linked the supposed playwright of Stratford to the sum of one thousand pounds.

10. Not much from Oxford's life helps to describe, four centuries later, his appearance and manner. Miller (2:407–9) and Ogburn (470) analyze the painted portraits. Ward analyzes the Hollar drawing of Queen Elizabeth with a man thought to be Oxford (appendix K).

11. The conflicting evidence about Oxford's burial is discussed by Miller (2:31). No will has been found, leading to Oxfordian speculation that it was confiscated by the ruling powers concerned about what it contained.

12. The associations between Oxford's three daughters and the men probably most responsible for the publication of the *First Folio*, namely Ben Jonson and the earls of Pembroke and Montgomery, are described by Miller in chapter 1 of volume 2.

CHAPTER 8: THE CASE FOR OXFORD AS AUTHOR

1. The moot court in Washington was reported in a major article by James Lardner in *The New Yorker* of April 11, 1988. For the moot court in London, see the *New York Times*, November 27, 1990, C21.

2. Justice Stevens's article appeared in the *University of Pennsylvania Law Review* 140, no. 4 (April 1992). Ogburn reports the views of Justices Powell and Blackmun in his second edition (1992), page vi. The third justice on the moot court in Washington was William J. Brennan, Jr.

3. McCullough writes in his foreword to Ogburn's book that Oxford as Shakespeare is "wholly believable." Sheed raises the possibility of "a closet lord" as Shakespeare in his review of *Shylock* by John Gross (*The New Yorker*, July 12, 1993, 99). Fadiman counts himself a convert on the

jacket of Ogburn's book. Basso reviewed five Shakespeare biographies in *The New Yorker* of April 8, 1950, found them wanting, and said the mysteries about Shakespeare "are mysteries no longer if the man we know as Shakespeare was really Edward de Vere." Galsworthy called Looney's book "the best detective story I have ever read" and gave copies to his friends (Miller, 1:648). Freud's interest is detailed by Miller (2:264–73).

4. Arguments for Lord Oxford have sometimes drawn allegations of social snobbery. Even if it were true, it would not affect the evidence, which can be evaluated whatever the motivation. The accusation can also cut against the Stratfordian's own man. If snobbery is the fawning desire to be associated with a higher social class, then Will Shakspere himself would be a classic example, ingratiating himself with the earl of Southampton with dedications, mingling with the nobility to pick up their manners and mores, and seeking a coat of arms to rise from commoner to gentleman (see Taylor, 218). Inverted snobbery might also be suspected on the part of some Stratfordians who adopt an extremely proletarian position, preferring the commoner and rejecting the idea that an aristocrat could be a literary genius, despite examples such as Count Tolstoy and Lord Byron, and other writers from aristocratic families, such as Pierre de Ronsard, James Boswell, and Joseph Conrad. The aristocracy has produced few artists of genius, but the aristocracy is a tiny fraction of the total population.

5. The only fully drawn characters in all of Shakespeare who are not of noble birth are Falstaff, Shylock, and Iago. Iago is the personification of evil and hardly a reflection of the author's views of life. Shylock, too, is an observed character, who does in fact have some redeeming qualities. Falstaff is Sir John, a bridging character who was accepted (elevated?) by Prince Hal to an ad hoc gentility (see Ogburn, 253ff.).

6. Northrop Frye, *On Shakespeare* (New Haven: Yale University Press, 1986, 10).

7. For the text of John Davies's poem, see Appendix A.

8. In *Shakespeare and Ovid* (Oxford: Clarendon Press, 1993), Jonathan Bate says: "For a long time it has been widely agreed that Shakespeare's favorite classical author, probably his favorite author in any language, was Publius Ovidius Naso" (vii).

9. On Arthur Golding, see Louis Thorn Golding's biography, *An Elizabethan Puritan, the Translator of Ovid's Metamorphoses and also of John Calvin's Sermons* (New York: Richard R. Smith, 1937, 29–36, and chap. 15, "Golding and Shakespeare").

10. On Shakespeare's knowledge of law, see John Lord Campbell, *Shakespeare's Legal Acquirements Considered* (New York: Appleton, 1859,

134), and Ogburn (296–301). For a summary of contrary views, see O. Hood Phillips, *Shakespeare and the Lawyers* (London: Methuen, 1972). Most lawyers agree that Shakespeare knew the law well, but disagree on whether he was trained in the law and knew more than did some other playwrights.

11. Among the lawyers who have written on Shakespeare biography are Nicholas Rowe, Lewis Theobold, Edmund Malone, James Boswell the younger, Joseph C. Hart, John Campbell Lord Chief Justice, Lord Penzance Queen's Counsel, Sir G. George Greenwood, Charlton Ogburn, Sr., Judge Minos Miller, and Ruth Loyd Miller. Richard Bentley, an editor of the *American Bar Association Journal*, contributed two articles to *Shakespeare Cross-Examination*, published by the ABA. (See Ruth Loyd Miller, "Lawyers as Shakespearean Scholars," unpublished paper, 1991.)

12. For Oxford's patronage of Lyly and other dramatists, see Ward (184, 197, 264).

13. Charlotte C. Stopes, *The Life of Henry, Third Earl of Southampton, Shakespeare's Patron* (Cambridge: University Press, 1922) is the standard life. Stopes spent seven years on research without finding any connection between the earl and Will Shakspere, and considered her life's work a failure. See also Bentley (155), Ward (313), and Ogburn (333).

14. The Shakespearean botanist is Leo H. Grindon, who wrote *The Shakspere Flora: A Guide to All the Principal Passages in Which Mention is Made of Trees, Plants, Flowers, and Vegetable Productions, With Comments and Botanical Particulars* (Manchester: Palmer and Howe, 1883).

15. Harrison, 4–5.

16. In *The Medical Mind of Shakespeare* (Sydney: Williams and Wilkins Addis, 1986), A. C. Kahl writes: "Shakespeare's plays bear witness to a profound knowledge of contemporary physiology and psychology, and he employed medical terms in a manner which would have been beyond the powers of any ordinary playwright or physician" (13–14). Medical journals have published several articles by a variety of specialists about Shakespeare's knowledge of medicine. In 1988 Dr. Lance Fogan, a California physician, won an award for the best research paper in the *Journal of the American Academy of Neurology*. "Shakespeare's medical knowledge was astounding," Fogan told an interviewer. "Centuries later, his description of characters is so accurate that physicians can diagnose them." His paper analyzed symptoms described by Shakespeare for a dozen neurological conditions, including Othello's apparent epilepsy (*Washington Post*, June 3, 1989). Will Shakspere's son-in-law was a practicing physician, but he left no mention of his father-in-law.

17. Pallas Athena's sobriquet was "Hasti-vibrans," the spear-shaker

(Ogburn, 97, 597, 729). Oxfordians also cite an address in Latin by Gabriel Harvey to Oxford before the queen in which Harvey is supposed to have said, "thy countenance shakes spears." Andrew Hannas of Purdue University has questioned the translation (*Shakespeare Oxford Society Newsletter* 29, no. 1B [Winter 1993]). But he goes on to find a "greatly reverberating pun" in the same passage that refers to Oxford's "unacknowledged theatrical involvement."

CHAPTER 9: OXFORD'S LIFE SPAN AND DATING THE PLAYS

1. For the Stratfordian dating, see principally Evans's chapter and table in the *Riverside Shakespeare* (47ff.); also the Pelican edition (19). The *Oxford Shakespeare* prints the plays "in a newly considered chronological order" (according to the jacket copy), but without much explanation; see page 1 for *Two Gentlemen*. Bevington (2, 32). Alexander, less precise, says simply that "Shakespeare must have been working as a dramatist for some years before 1590" (14). Oxfordian scholars generally have not attempted a full chronology (Ogburn, 771ff., esp. 779n; also 382ff.).

2. Individual authorities also suggest dates for the first play: A. S. Cairncross puts *Hamlet* in 1588 (*The Problem of Hamlet: A Solution* [London: Macmillan, 1936, xvi, 49, 179]); and Peter Levi puts *Titus Andronicus* in 1589 or 1590 (54–55).

3. For Schoenbaum's seven early plays, see *Compact Life*, 164.

4. Shakespeare's vocabulary, as demonstrated in his works, is the largest of any writer. It is conservatively estimated to have been at least fifteen thousand to eighteen thousand words, twice that used by the erudite classicist John Milton, who came just after Shakespeare; and Shakespeare is thought to have coined more than three thousand words (Ogburn, 291–93, citing Alfred Hart).

5. For the popularity of *Venus and Adonis* and *The Rape of Lucrece*, see the *Riverside Shakespeare* (1704, 1720).

6. Francis Meres is discussed more fully in chapter 11.

7. For a leading Oxfordian's views on dating the plays, see Ogburn (382–90).

8. For Oxford's withdrawal from public life and Shakespeare's emergence, see Looney, who calls it the beginning of Oxford's "Shakespearean period" (311). Looney describes the abrupt cessation of quarto publication of the plays for four years after Oxford's death in 1604 (352–53). The four quartos issued from 1605 to 1623 were *Lear* (1608), *Troilus and Cressida* (1609), *Pericles* (1609), and *Othello* (1622).

9. For Clark's dating, see her preface and part I, "The Problem

Stated," and chapters on the plays. See also Ogburn, who, among others, does not accept all of Clark's analysis (461).

10. For Schoenbaum's quip about "cunning parallels," which he calls a "discommoding truth," see *Lives* (437).

CHAPTER 10: OXFORD REVEALED IN SHAKESPEARE'S PLAYS

The allusions cited in this chapter are a sampling of those that appear to apply specifically and directly to Oxford. Ogburn and Ogburn cite hundreds that are more subtle, although the cumulative effect is powerful. Clark emphasizes the many hidden allusions in the plays to people and political/literary events in Oxford's life. For many, the 154 sonnets, as highly personal statements, most convincingly point to Oxford as the author (Looney, chap. 15; Ogburn, chap. 17).

1. For the Gad's Hill incident (*Henry IV Part 1*, act 2), see Ward (90), Ogburn and Ogburn (77, 713ff.), and Ogburn (528–29).

2. Shakespeare indulged constantly in punning and wordplay, and Oxfordians are convinced he left clues to his authorship in wordplay on his family name, Edward de Vere. The words "ever" and "every" can often be read as wordplay alluding to the author's name as E. Vere. A leading example is the headline for the unsigned advertisement that precedes *Troilus and Cressida*: "A never writer to an ever reader. News." (*Riverside Shakespeare*, 492). Oxfordians read this also as "an E. Vere writer to an E. Vere reader." Otherwise, its meaning is most obscure. The line "That *ever* I was born" is given both to Autolycus in *The Winter's Tale* and to Hamlet. In a multilingual pun, the title of *The Winter's Tale* translates to Le Conte d'Hiver in French, which sounds like "the count (i.e., earl) de Vere." During the Gad's Hill escapade, Prince Hal plans to trick Falstaff: "it would be argument for a week, laughter for a month and a good jest for *ever*." That is, a good jest for E. Vere (*Henry IV Part 1*, 2.2.96). Sonnet 76 asks (italics added):

> Why write I still all one, *ever* the same,
> And keep invention in a noted weed,
> That *every* word doth almost tell my name,
> Showing their birth, and where they did proceed?

"Every word" can also be read as an anagram for "Ver Edword."

3. *All's Well That Ends Well* is one of three plays not found in any records before its publication in the *First Folio*—no quarto edition, no

registration, no performance record, no mention by contemporaries. And, it is one of two plays (with *Hamlet*) that contain the most open and direct parallels to Oxford's life.

4. The Pelican edition of *All's Well* (1980) includes an introduction by Professor Jonas A. Barish that illuminates the difficulties scholars have found in this "rather nasty play" (14–15).

5. The early reference to the bed trick was found by Charles W. Barrell (reported by Ogburn, 576–79).

6. For the street fighting with Knyvet's men, see Ogburn (650) and an article by Gwynneth Bowen in Miller (2:85–94).

7. For the parallels to Oxford's life in *The Merchant of Venice*, see Ogburn (603), Ogburn and Ogburn (227–42), Ward (237), and Charles W. Barrell in Clark (345–48).

8. As a name, Shylock is an original. Stratfordian scholars have searched for its origins, but "it remains a mystery" for John Gross, author of *Shylock: A Legend and Its Legacy* (New York: Simon & Schuster, 1992, 63). Allan Bloom with Harry V. Jaffa say "its origin can only be conjectured," but they suggest Shelah (pronounced sh-lach), a name in a 1582 version of the *Old Testament* that is associated with the Tower of Babel (*Shakespeare's Politics* [Chicago: University of Chicago Press, 1964, 33n]).

9. *Hamlet* as autobiographical: "Everyone sees that he is the most autobiographical of all the characters," says Rowse (*Biography*, 321). "There is more of Shakespeare himself in this play than in any of his others," concludes Harrison (604). "Closer to Shakespeare than any other of his protagonists, Hamlet has depths, not easily sounded," writes Fraser (120). For the parallels in *Hamlet*, see Ogburn (357ff.), Ogburn and Ogburn (651ff.).

10. Oxford's stepfather, Charles Tyrell, bore a name that would have evil resonance for the author of *Richard III*. In the history play, Tyrell arranged for the murder of the two young princes in the Tower of London.

11. "Many scholars have argued that Burghley is being satirized as Polonius in *Hamlet*," according to *The Reader's Encyclopedia of Shakespeare* (90). "Burghley was certainly a Polonius," says Rowse the stalwart Stratfordian (*The Man*, 163). The resemblance of Polonius to Burghley was reported in 1869 by G. R. French (article by J. V. Miller in Miller, 2:430). J. V. Miller also details Burghley's nicknames (Miller, 2: 431–32).

12. The significant role of the book *Cardanus Comforte* in *Hamlet* was first proposed in 1839, nearly a century before the book's sponsor, Oxford, was suggested as Shakespeare (Miller, 2:497; Ogburn, 525).

13. For Horatio Vere and his brother, Francis, "the fighting Veres," see Ogburn (539, 561, 763), and Ward (126).

14. The longest version of *Hamlet*, at 3,800 lines, is the second quarto of 1604–1605, printed, as it happens, shortly after Oxford died in June 1604. Textual editors conclude that it was typeset from the author's own manuscript, although the compositors did a poor job (*Riverside Shakespeare*, 1186; *Oxford Shakespeare*, 653). Oxfordians conjecture that Horatio Vere may indeed have heeded the plea of Hamlet-as-Oxford "to tell my story" (5.2.339–348) and given the manuscript to the printers. (Records from 1604–5 have Will Shakspere lodging with the Mountjoy family in London, suing a Stratford man for payment of a loan of less than two pounds, and purchasing tithes in Stratford for the enormous sum of 440 pounds.)

CHAPTER 11: OBJECTIONS TO OXFORD AS SHAKESPEARE

1. The PBS "Frontline" program was "The Shakespeare Mystery," broadcast April 18, 1989, and December 22, 1992.

2. The authorship controversy is taken seriously by Professor Marjorie Garber of Harvard in *Shakespeare's Ghostwriters* (New York: Methuen, 1987), but not to resolve it. Garber's only interest is to determine why the question persists (chap. 1). Her objective is "to explore the significance of the debate itself, to consider the ongoing existence of the polemic between the pro-Stratford-lifers and pro-choice advocates as an exemplary literary event in its own right" (3). For her the plays themselves dramatize the questions raised in the authorship controversy:

> Shakespeare is a concept—and a construct—rather than an author. . . . The Ghost [in *Hamlet*] is Shakespeare. He is the one who comes as a revenant, belatedly instated, regarded as originally authoritative, rather than retrospectively and retroactively canonized, and deriving increased authority from this very instatement of authority backward, over time. (175–76)

3. The first book-length critique of the case for Oxford was by Irvin Matus in 1994. Until then, Oxford was usually lumped with Bacon, Marlowe, Derby, and the other candidates; and all in general were found wanting. One of the better analyses was in the *Atlantic Monthly* (October 1991), which devoted its cover and five articles to the debate, including two by Matus and two for Oxford by Tom Bethel. *The New Yorker* (November 4, 1988) covered the moot court debate in 1987 before three justices of the U.S. Supreme Court. In the mid-1970s, Professors Levin and Evans offered a rebuttal in *Harvard Magazine* (February 1975) of an article there by Ogburn (November 1974) on the case for Oxford. In his

book, Ogburn provides a counter-refutation to the Levin/Evans rebuttal, which he shows had mostly skirted his main arguments. The issue was debated by lawyers and others in *Shakespeare Cross-Examination* (1961), a collection of articles that had appeared in the *ABA Journal*. Books by Martin, Montague, Gibson, Wadsworth, and Churchill offer some objections to Oxford (see bibliography).

    4. The literacy rate is analyzed by David Cressy in *Literacy and the Social Order: Reading and Writing in Tudor and Stuart England* (Cambridge: Cambridge University Press, 1980, 176) and *Education in Tudor and Stuart England* (London: Arnold, 1975, 9).

    5. On censorship, see Annabel Patterson, *Censorship and Interpretation: The Conditions of Writing and Reading in Early Modern England* (Madison: University of Wisconsin Press, 1984, 53, 57). Although she is an ardent Stratfordian, Oxfordians generally agree with Patterson's main point. She argues throughout that

> the unstable but unavoidable relationship between writers and the holders of power was creative of a set of conventions that both sides partially understood and could partly articulate: conventions as to how far a writer could go in explicit address to the contentious issues of the day, and how, if he did *not* choose the confrontational approach, he could encode his opinions so that nobody would be *required* to make an example of him. (12; emphasis in original)

    6. To help explain the open secret of Oxford's authorship, some Oxfordians suggest that in his early twenties Oxford and Queen Elizabeth, seventeen years older, had a son. This birth to the "Virgin Queen" was concealed and he was raised by friends as their own son, the third earl of Southampton. If so, this could explain the devoted language of Shakespeare's (i.e., Oxford's), dedications to Southampton in the two narrative poems and suggest the identity of the young man addressed in the *Sonnets* with such love and devotion. Southampton would have been heir to the throne, although illegitimate unless Elizabeth and Oxford had secretly married. Oxfordians are divided on the issue. See Ogburn and Ogburn (817, 821ff.), and Ogburn (349, 519, 523). Sears makes the case for it in *Shakespeare and the Tudor Rose*; Hope and Holston (131) offer opposing views.

    7. On the application of the Shakespeare pseudonym to Will Shakspere, see Ogburn (192, 745).

    8. For Schoenbaum's "principal drawback," see *Lives* (433). *Lives* also contains his putdown of the case for Oxford (430–44).

    9. Scholars differ on the number of plays first staged after Oxford's

death. Schoenbaum says ten; the *Britannica* fourteen, possibly based on the *Riverside Shakespeare* chronology. Looney, Clark, and Ogburn and Ogburn provide Oxfordian chronologies in summary form. The three plays not in any records before publication in the *First Folio* of 1623 are *Coriolanus, Timon of Athens,* and *All's Well That Ends Well.*

10. The controversy over the line in *The Tempest* (1.2.226–29) is covered by Miller (1:438); Ogburn (388); Miller again in *The Shakespeare Newsletter* (Spring 1990, 12), and by Roe in *The Shakespeare Newsletter* (Fall-Winter 1989, 36). The etymology of "Bermoothes" is detailed by E. E. Sugden in *A Topological Dictionary to the Works of Shakespeare and His Fellow Dramatists* (Manchester: Manchester University Press, 1925, 58); he cites references in Ben Jonson's works around 1614 to the Bermudas in London. A modern sketch-map of London in the 1570s showing the "Bermudas" near Charing Cross is at the front of *Ben Jonson: A Life* by David Riggs (Cambridge: Harvard University Press, 1989).

11. Meres's list of poets and playwrights is given by the *Riverside Shakespeare* (1844) and by Bentley (199ff.). See also Looney (quoted by Miller, 1:657ff.), Schoenbaum (*Compact Life,* 189–92), and Ogburn (195–96).

12. For Matus on Meres, see *Atlantic Monthly* (October 1991, 79), and Matus's book (151).

13. For "other objections," see books in the final section of the bibliography, including Churchill (204).

14. For the comment by Henry James, see Ogburn (181) and Hope and Holston (chap. 4). The Shakespeare quote is from *Measure for Measure* (5.1.45); Oxford's from a letter dated May 7, 1603. Fowler (770–76) cites eight places in the plays where Shakespeare, like Oxford, says "truth is truth" or some close variation, and many more instances of plays on the words true and truth. The de Vere family's motto was "Vero nihil verius" (nothing truer than truth).

Select, Annotated Bibliography for Further Reading

This bibliography is intended as a guide for further reading and study. Almost all the works are from the twentieth century. Many of them have excellent bibliographies, and are so noted. The criteria for inclusion were whether the book is authoritative and influential, whether it is available in stores or libraries or by mail, and whether it is well written and relatively up-to-date. Many other books that were consulted, but not included here, are noted in the text and notes.

THE PRINCIPAL OXFORDIAN WORKS

The single most important book is Charlton Ogburn's *The Mysterious William Shakespeare: The Myth and the Reality,* published in 1984, with a second edition in 1992. Ruth Loyd Miller's two volumes include Looney's pioneer book and a wealth of additional material.

Looney, J. Thomas. *"Shakespeare" Identified in Edward de Vere, the Seventeenth Earl of Oxford.* 3d ed. Edited by Ruth Loyd Miller, with additional material. Jennings, LA 70546–1309: Minos Publishing, 1975. A classic, landmark book, first published in London in 1920 by Cecil Palmer (2d ed. New York: Duell, Sloan and Pearce, 1949, with an introduction by William McFee and afterword by Charles Wisner Barrell). Miller's edition also includes *The Poems of Edward de Vere, Seventeenth Earl of Oxford,* with Looney's introduction and notes. Available by telephone order from Minos Publishing (318–824–4580) as the first of a two-volume set edited by Miller.

Miller, Ruth Loyd, ed. *Oxfordian Vistas.* Jennings, LA 70546–1309: Minos Publishing, 1975. The second volume of her two-volume set, which collects scores of articles, many by Miller, plus letters and excerpts on twenty-five topics of interest to Oxfordians.

Ogburn, Charlton. *The Mysterious William Shakespeare: The Myth and the Reality.* 2d ed. McLean, VA 22101: EPM Publications, 1992. Foreword by David McCullough, author of *Truman.* The most influential book that makes the case for Oxford as Shakespeare; thorough and detailed in more than eight hundred pages, and eminently readable. Excellent bibliography and a useful chronology showing in adjacent columns for each year the events in the lives of Oxford and Will Shakspere, dates of Shakespeare's works, and related events.

Ogburn, Dorothy, and Charlton Ogburn. *This Star of England: William Shake-speare, Man of the Renaissance.* New York: Coward-McCann, 1952. A retelling of Oxford's life in 1,270 pages based on the many examples of connections the authors found between his life and the works of Shakespeare. The authors were the parents of Charlton Ogburn (above).

Ogburn, Dorothy, and Charlton Ogburn, Jr. *Shake-speare, the Man Behind the Name.* New York: Morrow, 1962. The book compares Oxford and Will Shakspere on crucial points, such as evidence of apprenticeship as an author, and includes a Stratfordian rejoinder followed by a counter-rejoinder. Short and instructive, but hard to find.

Ward, Bernard M. *The Seventeenth Earl of Oxford, 1550–1604, from Contemporary Records.* London: Murray, 1928. The only full-length biography of Oxford, the book is by an Oxfordian who decided to set aside his view that Oxford wrote Shakespeare and limit his purview strictly to the historical record, omitting any of the links to Shakespeare. Available from Minos Publishing in copyrighted photocopy format.

OTHER SIGNIFICANT OXFORDIAN AND NON-STRATFORDIAN WORKS

Clark, Eva Turner. *Hidden Allusions in Shakespeare's Plays: A Study of the Oxford Theory Based on the Records of Early Court Revels and Personalities of the Times.* Edited by Ruth Loyd Miller, with introduction and additional notes. Jennings, LA 70546-1309: Minos Publishing, 1974. First published by Cecil Palmer in London, 1930, as *Shakespeare's Plays in the Order of Their Writing.* Excellent summary in Clark's preface and introduction. Clark dates the plays much earlier, based on topical allusions and on the entry dates of eleven anonymous, lost plays of the 1570s that have titles similar to Shakespeare's plays. Not all Oxfordians agree with Clark.

The Elizabethan Review. Edited and published twice a year by Gary B. Goldstein, 123–60 83rd Ave., Kew Gardens, NY 11415. Articles, reviews and letters on matters Elizabethan and Oxfordian.

Fowler, William Plumer. *Shakespeare Revealed in Oxford's Letters.* Portsmouth, NH: Randall, 1986. Thousands of parallels in language found in thirty-seven letters by Oxford and the works of Shakespeare. Some are impressive.

Greenwood, G. George. *The Shakespeare Problem Restated.* London: John Lane/The Bodley Head, 1908. The classic, complete formulation of the case against Will Shakspere as the author by a British lawyer and member of Parliament who looks on it as a matter of evidence and reasonable probability. Greenwood does not try to determine who might have been the author.

———. *Is There a Shakespeare Problem?* London: John Lane/The Bodley Head, 1916. Another sally, rebutting critics of his earlier book.

Hope, Warren, and Kim Holston. *The Shakespeare Controversy: An Analysis of the Claimants to Authorship, and Their Champions and Detractors.* Jefferson, NC: McFarland, 1992. A short survey of the nineteenth-century claimants, Looney's background and work, and the authorship controversy. Extensive annotated bibliography of works famous and obscure, by year.

Sears, Elisabeth. *Shakespeare and the Tudor Rose.* Seattle: Consolidated Press, 1990. On Oxford's relations with Queen Elizabeth I and whether the third earl of Southampton was their son. Ogburn and Hope/Holston offer comments on this theory.

Shakespeare Oxford Society Newsletter. Edited since the late 1980s by Morse Johnson of Cincinnati. Quarterly newsletter with scholarly articles, reviews, commentary, and correspondence. Subscriptions from the society at 7D Taggart Dr., Nashua, NH 03060.

Twain, Mark. *Is Shakespeare Dead? From My Autobiography.* New York: Harper & Brothers, 1909. A rollicking description of Twain's long-standing doubts that Will Shakspere was the author.

SOURCES GIVING BOTH SIDES OF THE ISSUE

Atlantic Monthly. "Looking for Shakespeare: Two Partisans Explain and Debate the Authorship Question." October 1991. Five articles in all, including the case for Oxford by Tom Bethell, Washington editor of *The American Spectator*, the case for "Shakespeare" by Irvin Matus, an independent scholar, and rejoinders by both.

Gregory, Tappan, ed. *Shakespeare Cross-Examination*. Chicago: Cuneo Press, 1961. Ten articles by lawyers and others that had appeared in several issues of the *American Bar Association Journal*, plus letters to the editor. Gregory says, "The problem is not merely a literary one; the question of the identity of the author of the plays is also one of evidence, and therefore within the province of lawyers."

Hunt, Douglas. *The Riverside Guide to Writing*. Boston: Houghton Mifflin, 1991. An analysis of the authorship controversy in an unusual setting, a book on writing. Chapter 6, "Arguing When Facts Are Disputed," uses Mark Twain's objections to the conventional attribution as a case study "to evaluate the effectiveness of arguments for and against the thesis that the man named Shakespeare actually wrote the works attributed to him."

McMichael, George, and E. M. Glenn. *Shakespeare and His Rivals: A Casebook in the Authorship Controversy*. New York: Odyssey Press, 1962. Valuable for its collection of articles and book excerpts on the authorship question, with emphasis on Marlowe as a claimant; designed for a college course.

PBS-TV. "The Shakespeare Mystery," a "Frontline" TV program broadcast on April 18, 1989, and December 22, 1992. Schoenbaum, Rowse, et al. speak for Will Shakspere; Ogburn, Lord Burford, and J. Enoch Powell for Oxford. Available on cassette (1–800–328–PBS1).

Reed, J. D. "Some Ado About Who Was, or Was Not Shakespeare." *Smithsonian*, September 1987. Reed, a poet, novelist, and creative writing teacher, based his article largely on Ogburn.

COLLECTED WORKS OF SHAKESPEARE, WITH INTRODUCTIONS THAT INCLUDE BIOGRAPHICAL INFORMATION

Most students and readers of Shakespeare get their biographical information from the introductions to the collected works and to individual editions of the plays. The biographies they find there are all Stratfordian. The question of the author's identity, when mentioned, is noted briefly and dismissed. Harbage, Harrison, and the *Oxford Shakespeare* ignore it completely; Craig and the *Riverside Shakespeare* barely mention it; Bevington gives its history but does not address the case for Oxford. Some individual editions of the plays provide brief Stratfordian biographies (e.g., Folger, Pelican, Signet); others nothing (e.g., Arden, Oxford, New Cambridge).

Alexander, Peter, ed. *William Shakespeare: The Complete Works*. London: Collins, 1951. Alexander accepts the story that Shakespeare was a schoolmaster and goes on from there.

Bevington, David, ed. *The Complete Works of Shakespeare*. 4th ed. New York: HarperCollins, 1992. A long and informative general introduction includes a standard Stratfordian biography and six paragraphs (lxi) on "The Anti-Stratfordian Movement." Appendix 1 provides several paragraphs on dating and sources for each play. This fourth edition is the successor to Craig's edition.

Craig, Harden, ed. *The Complete Works of Shakespeare*. Chicago: Scott, Foresman, 1951.

Evans, G. Blakemore, textual ed.; Harry Levin, general introduction; et al. *The Riverside Shakespeare*. Boston: Houghton Mifflin, 1974. This volume offers a generous selection of records, literary allusions, and commentary from Shakespeare's time, including a facsimile of the entire prefatory material to the *First Folio*. Especially valuable is a Stratfordian chronology of the plays "according to the most commonly accepted date or dates," with comments on the records and derived sources.

Harbage, Alfred, ed. *William Shakespeare: The Complete Works*. New York: Viking Penguin, 1977. General introduction by Frank W. Wadsworth.

Harrison, G. B., ed. *Shakespeare: Major Plays and the Sonnets*. New York: Harcourt Brace, 1948.

Wells, Stanley, and Gary Taylor, eds. *William Shakespeare: The Complete Works, Compact Edition*. Oxford: Clarendon Press, 1988. Introduction by Wells. Its nickname is the *Oxford Shakespeare*, and wits note that if Oxford is ever accepted as the true author the name should be changed to "the Oxford Oxford."

THE PRINCIPAL STRATFORDIAN WORKS

Only the reader with exceptional fortitude could tolerate more than three or four of the many full-length biographies of Will Shakspere of Stratford. Two or three accounts of his mundane life are enough, and sorting fact from conjecture is wearying after a while. If a choice had to be made, it might include Schoenbaum's *Compact Life*, Bentley, Wilson, and Rowse or Chute. All are relatively short and quite readable. Schoenbaum, the most prominent biographical authority and defender of the

Stratfordian faith in the late twentieth century, overshadows all the others with four major works.

Bentley, G. E. *Shakespeare: A Biographical Handbook*. New Haven: Yale University Press, 1961. A short, sober biography with useful detail on Meres in chapter 8, "Shakespeare's Reputation."

Brown, Ivor. *Shakespeare*. New York: Time, Inc., 1949. A paperback biography of "the Warwickshire Wonder" with "the Hand of Glory." Chapter 15 addresses the anti-Stratfordians in general.

Brown, Ivor, and George Fearon. *This Shakespeare Industry: Amazing Monument*. New York: Harper & Brothers, 1939. Not a biography as such, but a wry account of Stratford-on-Avon's growth as "the Birthplace" and the Bard's apotheosis as a paying concern.

Chambers, E. K. *William Shakespeare: A Study of Facts and Problems*. 2 vols. Oxford: Clarendon Press, 1930. A careful examination of nearly all the Stratfordian and Shakespearean documents, by one of the half dozen leading Shakespearean scholars of all time; plus the text of most of them and a short narrative biography. An invaluable reference tool.

Chute, Marchette. *Shakespeare of London*. New York: Dutton, 1949. A biography that was widely read and well received. Oxfordians suggest that it offers much more about the London of Shakespeare than Shakespeare of London.

Fraser, Russell. *Young Shakespeare*. New York: Columbia University Press, 1988. The first of a two-volume personal and impressionistic view of Will Shakspere as a pragmatic businessman and professional playwright.

———. *Shakespeare: The Later Years*. New York: Columbia University Press, 1992. The second of two volumes.

Kay, Dennis. *Shakespeare: His Life, Work and Era*. New York: Morrow, 1992. A biography set in the context of the age, with much more on the works and the era than the life.

Lee, Sidney. *A Life of Shakespeare*. New York: Macmillan, 1924. A revised and expanded edition of the original 1898 biography by the man who wrote the entry for Will Shakspere in the *Dictionary of National Biography*. Ironically, Lee also wrote the entry for Edward de Vere, seventeenth earl of Oxford, but without realizing, of course, that Oxford would become the leading candidate for authorship within the century. Both entries are worth consulting.

Levi, Peter. *The Life and Times of William Shakespeare*. New York: Holt, 1988. A biography "in the context of the times," with much conjecture.

Rowse, A. L. *William Shakespeare: A Biography*. New York: Harper &

Row, 1963. A reverential Stratfordian biography by a staunch and entirely self-confident defender.

———. *Shakespeare the Man*. Rev. ed. New York: St. Martin's Press, 1973. Another biography from the historian who presents new insights with "unanswerable certainty."

Schoenbaum, S. *William Shakespeare: A Documentary Life*. New York: Oxford University Press, 1975. An oversized, expensive volume of 273 pages, elegantly printed, with many facsimile reproductions of documents—some of them fold-outs—from Will Shakspere's life.

———. *William Shakespeare: A Compact Documentary Life*, rev. ed. with a new postscript. New York: Oxford University Press, 1987. A cheaper, more convenient paperback edition of the oversize *Documentary Life*.

———. *Shakespeare: His Life, His Language, His Theater*. New York: Penguin Signet, 1990. Two chapters of biography, plus chapters on Shakespeare's English, the theaters, other playwrights, and on his poems and plays.

———. *Shakespeare's Lives*, new edition. New York: Oxford University Press, 1991. A history of the immense biographical scholarship devoted to Will Shakspere of Stratford over the centuries. In Schoenbaum's words, "a novel species of Shakespearean biography, with the protagonist gradually emerging from the mists of ignorance and misconception, to be seen through a succession of different eyes and from constantly shifting vantage points." It includes a full section on other claimants to authorship, including Oxford, but without addressing the major arguments for him.

The Shakespeare Newsletter. Edited by Thomas A. Pendleton and John W. Mahon and published quarterly by the English department at Iona College, New Rochelle, NY 10801. Publishes reviews, news items, scholarly papers, and theater notes.

Taylor, Gary. *Reinventing Shakespeare: A Cultural History from the Restoration to the Present*. New York: Weidenfeld and Nicolson, 1989. Not a biography as such, but a lively history of Shakespeare's evolving reputation over 330 years, complementing Schoenbaum's *Lives*.

Wilson, Ian. *Shakespeare: The Evidence*. London: Headline, 1993. Another rendition of the Stratfordian story by the author of *Jesus: The Evidence*.

Wilson, J. Dover. *The Essential Shakespeare: A Biographical Adventure*. New York: Macmillan, 1935. Based in part on lectures, this slim Stratfordian book describes "the kind of man I believe Shakespeare to have been." Oxfordians appreciate some of his insights.

STRATFORDIAN BOOKS THAT DEFEND HIM AGAINST OTHER CLAIMANTS

Churchill, R. C. *Shakespeare and His Betters: A History and a Criticism of the Attempts Which Have Been Made to Prove That Shakespeare's Works Were Written by Others.* Bloomington: Indiana University Press, 1959. A curious title that seems to esteem claimants to authorship as Will Shakspere's "betters," presumably an attempt at sarcasm. The book summarizes the arguments for the major claimants, followed by the case against each. Chapter 9, "The Case Against Oxford and Others," objects mainly to shifting the dates of the plays back ten years.

Gibson, H. N. *The Shakespeare Claimants.* London: Methuen, 1962. A defense of Will Shakspere against claims for Bacon, Derby, Marlowe, and Oxford considered as a leader of a group of writers.

Hill, Frank E. *To Meet Will Shakespeare.* New York: Dodd Mead, 1949. A fictionalized biography complete with imagined dialogue, but including a twenty-eight-page postscript, "The Imposters," that refutes Oxford as the author.

Martin, Milward W. *Was Shakespeare Shakespeare? A Lawyer Reviews the Evidence.* New York: Cooper Square, 1965. An answer to the Oxfordian articles in Gregory, *Shakespeare Cross-Examination.*

Matus, Irvin. *Shakespeare, in Fact.* New York: Continuum, 1994. The first book-length critique of Oxford as the author. Matus, an independent scholar, disputes many Oxfordian interpretations of primary source documents in his defense of Will Shakspere. Somewhat fragmented and recondite, the book includes material that appeared in his articles in *Atlantic Monthly* of October 1991.

Montague, W. K. *The Man of Stratford: The Real Shakespeare.* New York: Vantage Press, 1963. A point-by-point rebuttal of Ogburn and Ogburn (1952); Calvin Hoffman, *The Murder of the Man Who Was Shakespeare* (i.e., Christopher Marlowe; New York: Messner, 1955); and the Oxfordian articles in Gregory, *Shakespeare Cross-Examination.*

Robertson, J. M. *The Baconian Heresy: A Confutation.* London: Jenkins, 1913. A rebuttal of Twain and Greenwood, including a detailed denial of claims for Shakespeare's exceptional knowledge of the law.

Wadsworth, Frank W. *The Poacher from Stratford.* Berkeley: University of California, 1958. Largely a refutation of the Baconian theory, it dismisses claims for Oxford without examination. Curiously, the title seems to denigrate the Stratford man by alluding to his alleged deer-poaching (and play-poaching?).

Index

About the Author

RICHARD F. WHALEN is a writer, lecturer, and President of the Shakespeare Oxford Society. He has received degrees from Fordham College, the Sorbonne, and Yale Graduate School. After military service in France, he was a reporter and editor, principally with the Associated Press in New York, and for many years he was an executive in corporate communications at IBM. He now lives on Cape Cod, where he continues to write on the seventeenth earl of Oxford as the man behind the pseudonym "William Shakespeare."